KW-111-187

As free
as a bird

As free
as a bird
Peter Johnson

to Sonja

Patrick Stephens, Cambridge

©Peter Johnson 1976

All rights reserved. No part of this publication may be
reproduced, stored in a retrieval system or transmitted, in any
form or by any means, electronic, mechanical, photocopying,
recording or otherwise, without prior permission in writing
from Patrick Stephens Ltd

ISBN 0 85059 280 1

First published in Great Britain in 1977

First published in South Africa by C. Struik Publishers,
Cape Town
Published in Great Britain by Patrick Stephens Ltd, Bar Hill,
Cambridge, CB3 8EL

Foreword

Even as the birds which I have portrayed and which you will read about in this book have evolved and been changed by the forces of natural selection, so has this book run the gamut of modification, adaptation and improvement. So much so that the text is now, in its completed form, not only the work of many – and of the many I am the very least – but also differs from my original presentation as greatly as Archaeopteryx differs from the Antarctic Tern.

My debt, for the factual content, the incredible fascination and the living environmental context of those species of birds which I have chosen to represent, is wholly due to the Percy FitzPatrick Institute of African Ornithology at the University of Cape Town. Obviously my debt is specifically to the members of the Institute's staff, past and present, and in particular to Dr Jack Winterbottom for his help and for introducing me to my publisher.

This marriage between my wish to show the freedom, living and continual movement of my subjects on the one hand, and of on-going adaptive make-up with which a bird must be equipped to survive on the other, has resulted in a book which deliberately avoids being either a field guide or a scientific presentation of facts in support of some particular theory.

This book is intended to be readable and interesting and ideally, it can be picked up at any time, opened anywhere and enjoyed with the unconfined freedom of the birds I portray.

Contents

5	Foreword
7	The Sea and the Coast
47	Rivers and Vleis
108	The Veld
142	Trees and Woodland
195	Birds of the Riverine Forest
207	Index

The Sea and the Coast

Man has always regarded the sea as a symbol of purity and freedom; and so, in the past, it has been. But today there are clear signs of increasing pollution. On all the main traffic lanes criss-crossing the oceans the surface is littered with plastic debris, other waste, and streaked with slicks of oil – some of which ultimately washes up on the beaches. The area below the tide mark on many rocky coasts is festooned with tangles of nylon fishing line; broken bottles and tins lie scattered over the foreshore. These things naturally affect the living creatures of the sea. What is more, the degree to which the coast has already suffered clearly illustrates the urgent need for the rigorous enforcement of protective legislation.

Penguins

Birds, like man, are warm-blooded and must maintain a constant body temperature. The seabirds of southern Africa, and more particularly those of the western Atlantic coast, have had to evolve methods of regulating their body temperature in the face of two extremes: the cold Benguela Current on one hand, and the inexorable African sun on the other. Birds like the penguin have developed a way of life in which they seldom come ashore during the heat of the day except to nest and moult. And to cope with the chill waters in which they spend most of their lives, they are protected by a thick layer of body fat, densely-packed feathers and naked areas confined to beak and feet. Birds like the gannet that spend more time out of the water lose excess heat through their feet; others have areas of naked skin to assist the cooling process.

Waterbirds have a natural oil in their plumage which helps insulate them from the cold water by maintaining the structure of each feather and making it both air- and watertight. But the mineral oils and detergents that man uses and then thoughtlessly discards, destroy this; the structure of the plume breaks down and the bird becomes waterlogged. The layer of trapped air is lost and the bird, now robbed of its insulation, is driven ashore to escape the effects of the cold sea.

Of all birds, penguins are the most vulnerable to oil. Unable to fly, once in a slick they cannot escape and are forced to come ashore where there is no food for them. Furthermore, in trying to clean their feathers by preening they may swallow harmful or even lethal amounts of oil.

The Jackass Penguin gets its name from its love-call, which is very like the amorous bray of a donkey. At night when they come ashore to court, often in dense fog, this harsh sound keeps the birds in touch with one another and plays a prominent part in the nocturnal courtship.

The Jackass is southern Africa's only resident and breeding penguin, and its neat appearance makes it an attractive and apparently lovable bird – a sort of avian parody of humanity. It is as well, however, to warn sympathetic bird-lovers that the penguin does not reciprocate their affection and its beak can inflict a nasty bite.

Its breeding grounds are the offshore islands from Algoa Bay to southern South West Africa. The islands on which it breeds are also tenanted by vast flocks of cormorants and gannets which produce guano, a highly-prized natural fertilizer. Here, by choice, the penguin nests in burrows which it digs in the sand or under rocks. This it does for two reasons: to find protection from a harsh sun, and to protect its eggs and young from rapacious gulls and other predatory birds.

Penguins are largely fish-eaters, with a predilection for the shoal-living pilchards and anchovies which are basic to the fishing industry. Over-exploitation of fishing grounds threatens not only to ruin the fisheries, but also to deprive the penguin (as well as gannets and certain cormorants) of their food supply. In turn, any significant drop in the number of these birds would spell the end of the already declining guano industry.

Recent work on penguins suggests that they are more numerous than was thought – although on one or two small islands the population has undoubtedly been somewhat affected by oil spills. Cleansing of oil-soaked birds has been reasonably effective and has, in the process, shown that penguins are selective eaters. Their natural food contains oily matter not found in hake, for instance, and to keep captive birds in peak condition they must be fed the right kinds of fish. But valuable as rehabilitation is from a humanitarian point of view, it is likely that the number saved contributes little to the conservation of the species.

1 The penguin's true element is the sea; if and when it comes ashore it does so in the cool of the night as it is over-insulated for land-living. It swims using its flippers, as flying birds use their wings, to propel itself along with grace and speed. I have often marvelled at the sight of penguins coming ashore; their ability to avoid being tumbled by the breakers is an impressive exhibition of mastery over the surf.

2 Penguins are a very ancient group of birds, the oldest fossils dating back 40 or 50 million years. Even then they had already developed flippers and feet similar to those of penguins living today. What is more, except for one species on the Galapagos Islands, they are and always have been confined to the southern hemisphere.

3 In the early morning gloom hundreds of Jackass Penguins troop back to the sea. The penguin population has declined quite drastically over the last 50 years. At the turn of the century it was estimated in millions, but today they number only about 250 000. This is the result of a host of factors: bird and man competing for the same food source; guano scraping has made the nesting sites more hostile and breeding is therefore not necessarily successful; and oil spillage has undoubtedly had an adverse effect.

4 Decorating an offshore rock in silhouette, Cape Cormorants pause on their evening return to a nearby roost.

5 The White-breasted Cormorant's nest is far more substantial than that of the Cape Cormorant (see following page). On the barren offshore islands where the Cape species nests the birds not only compete with the hundreds of other members of the colony but also expend precious energy and time flying long distances in search of food, leaving them relatively little opportunity to search for nesting materials.

4

Cormorants

There are four species of cormorant that inhabit southern African shores and two of them are found on inland waters too. Most numerous is the Cape Cormorant. Indeed, the long graceful skeins of birds, flying low over the sea, are characteristic of Cape coasts.

The Cape Cormorant is gregarious: it not only nests in vast colonies, but assembles to roost as well. A spectacular example of this is the huge gathering that settles nightly on sandbanks just inside the Orange River mouth. This cormorant also prefers to fish in groups, diving into the water – sometimes giving a little jump for impetus – gliding underwater using its feet to propel itself until a fish is caught, and then surfacing. The fish is swallowed head first so that the spines slip down without catching on the bird's throat – not always an easy task to accomplish, and one often requiring odd contortions of neck and head. The bird then leap-frogs over its fellows and plunges in again at the head of the flock, repeating the sequence time after time. When joined, as they so often are, by penguins and plummeting flocks of gannets and terns, the ocean seems alive with hungry birds.

To many people the sight of these birds perched with wings outspread after fishing is a familiar one, and they have logically

concluded that they must be drying themselves. This is all the more plausible because the cormorant's plumage is more lightly waterproofed than, say, ducks' or penguins'. Recently, however, some doubt has been cast on the 'drying' hypothesis as it has been seen that cormorants also adopt this pose in the early morning before they start the day's fishing, and when the wings are still dry. Another theory is that they are simply warming themselves. Probably both assumptions are partially true, for there is no reason to suppose that wearing wet feathers is any less uncomfortable than wearing wet clothes.

Cormorants are extremely efficient fishers and as a result of their skills do not have to spend unduly long periods in the

water. In fact, the body insulation necessary to other diving birds is a hindrance where the cormorant is concerned for it adds unwanted buoyancy which some cormorants partially offset by swallowing pebbles as ballast.

Cape Cormorants nest in closely-packed colonies on the guano islands of the west coast and also on platforms specially built for them in relatively sheltered water to make guano collecting easier. With available space at a premium, there is fierce competition among breeding birds for suitable sites, but eventually the colony settles down with each nest just out of peck-range of its neighbours'. Nesting on relatively barren offshore islands has its disadvantages. To make an inviting spot on which to lay its eggs, the Cape Cormorant creates its nest out of much fought-over odds and ends, whatever vegetation it can find nearby, and seaweed – indeed, to search far and wide is a waste of precious energy and the Cape Cormorant's 'home' is a meagre affair. On the nest, when one of a pair joins its partner, they reinforce the pair-bond by indulging in a most curious display of wing-flapping, tail-cocking and yawning.

Every now and then some epidemic disease seems to sweep through the Cape Cormorant population. Affected birds – mainly juveniles – behave strangely, even flying inland before they die. When this happens they are heavily infested with lice, but this is more probably a symptom than the cause of the disease. It is notable that this epidemic invariably occurs immediately after the breeding season when there is considerable pressure on available food sources. Presumably the stricken birds are those already weakened by lack of food.

The White-breasted Cormorants are easily distinguished by their shimmering white underparts. I have often seen them at the coast, and also inland wherever there are fairly large stretches of permanent water. Although it has not yet been finally proven, it appears that the marine and freshwater dwellers do not mix – so far no White-breasted Cormorant ringed in fresh water has been recovered at sea.

Not only the White-breasted, but all species of cormorant with white underparts are largely confined to the southern hemisphere. A mystery exists for, in parts of Ethiopia, the two forms meet and interbreed with the all-black kind common to the area; yet no one knows why a bird, which is elsewhere entirely black, developed its splash of white only in the southern part of its range.

6 Choice not chance dictates Cape Cormorants' nesting sites in this crowded colony. Each spot is selected just out of its neighbour's pecking-range.

7 'Gular fluttering' is perfectly illustrated by this Reed Cormorant as it palpitates its throat. Rapidly drawing in and expelling air over its wet mouth and throat, the bird cools itself during the heat of the day.

7

8

9

8 Social birds that have to cover long distances often adopt a particular pattern of flight to conserve energy. Flapping both wings, each bird gains lift as a result of the air-stream generated by the wing-beat of the bird immediately ahead, and provides the same assistance for the one behind. By taking advantage of this slipstream and flying in a diagonal line, it need use less power than it would flying alone. The leader, however, must make his own headway, and to spread the load evenly the birds take turns in this position.

9 Preening cormorants groom their feathers in a comfort action.

10 The distinctiveness of the marine Crowned Cormorant and the freshwater Reed Cormorant gives rise to the argument that they are two species, not one. The Crowned Cormorant, as the photograph clearly shows, has a pronounced crest on the forehead which helps distinguish it from its freshwater relative, the Reed Cormorant, which lives on rivers, dams and even small pools. When young, and in the off-season the underparts of adult plumage are a rather dingy, dirty white – a poor facsimile of the White-breasted species' glossy feathers.

10

11 In the cold grey light of morning a fishing fleet shelters off Dassen Island while skeins of cormorants and gannets fly their separate ways.

12 Co-operative living brought to a fine art on a teeming gannet colony. The bird 'sky-pointing' (top left) adopts this appeasing pose to move unmolested among its neighbours. The dramatic black line of naked skin down the front of its throat emphasises the gesture.

11

Gannets

The third important denizen of the guano island community is the Cape Gannet which is so similar to its North Atlantic and Australasian relations that many ornithologists regard all three as races of a single species. Like the Cape Cormorant, it flies in groups strung low over the sea, though in somewhat smaller parties, and while it, too, feeds gregariously its method of doing so is entirely different. The fishing gannet flies along above the water, checks briefly, half-closes its wings and then plunges head-first into the sea. Although much of its food is captured close to the surface the force of its dive may carry it to a depth of more than 10 metres, protective cushions within its

13

13 Eyes on the look-out and calling to its mate in the colony below, the gannet pin-points its own nest by sight and sound before landing helicopter-like.

14 Piercing eyes at front are a distinctive feature of the gannet. Whereas most birds' eyes are set farther back on the head, the gannet's peer straight ahead to aid the depth perception crucial if this bird is to fish successfully.

breast and head absorbing some of the shock. A flock of gannets fishing is an exhilarating sight, and I often find myself on tenterhooks lest a plunging bird should collide with another rising from the water – but it never does.

The gannet's cup-shaped mud-and-guano nest is built just out of its neighbours' peck-range. The bird arrives immediately above it and descends directly, helicopter-like, but for take-off it requires a long run to gather speed before becoming airborne. In a densely-populated colony this is naturally impossible and the gannet must therefore make its way out on foot, treading circumspectly and in an appeasing manner if it is to escape a severe pecking from every bird it passes. With head and neck upstretched and beak 'sky-pointing' it indicates that

its intentions are non-aggressive. Then, once free, it runs to gain speed and eventually takes off.

During the breeding season gannets create such an uproar that they can be heard over a great distance. To the human ear this seems a senseless din but the gannet can isolate and pin-point the sound of its spouse or chicks in the teeming colony. As the bird approaches, its call is answered by its mate or young and in this way it quickly finds its nest.

While breeding, gannets perform a variety of ritualised gestures, perhaps the most spectacular of which involves fencing with the bill to reaffirm that they are indeed a pair. The two birds, with necks and heads stretched upwards, rub their beaks together as if sharpening them – though anyone who has had the misfortune to be pecked by a gannet will know that this is scarcely necessary! Another breeding peculiarity is that whereas most birds incubate their eggs against the breast, the gannet tucks its single egg snugly under its black webbed feet, blue toes holding it firmly in place. Indeed, it makes remarkable use of its feet, not only for walking, swimming and incubating, but also to regulate its temperature. In hot weather gannets cool themselves by paddling in their own excreta and on cold but clear days they will stand with their feet splayed out in the sun, warming them.

After the breeding season gannets disperse. The adult birds seldom move beyond the waters of southern Africa, but the young go much farther, on the west coast travelling as far as the Niger delta and on the east coast to Mozambique. One would expect all the young from the Algoa Bay colony to go to Mozambique but this is by no means the case as some of them round Cape Agulhas and move on up the west coast. This migration has been the subject of much conjecture but it is probably an attempt by the young to avoid competition for food with older birds. Gannet fledglings are distinguished by their brown feathers which give way at maturity to the distinctive adult plumage. They leave the nest with a considerable reserve of fat and, if they are to survive, must teach themselves to become proficient fishers before it is all used up.

Ornithologists travelling deep into the interior of West Africa were astonished to find local black people wearing necklaces of rings taken from gannets that had been shot and eaten. The scientists were able to make important findings from what had become treasured items of jewellery. These numbered and dated rings that are placed on the legs of birds have proved invaluable to researchers who use the data to trace the movements of various species and to learn something of their migratory habits.

Pelicans

One of nature's most comic creatures must surely be the pelican, either seen waddling pompously on the ground or preparing its ponderous body for take-off. With its wings flapping, its big feet punching frantically at the water as if tied together, it is indeed a preposterous sight, but once on the wing, majesty returns. With neck bent and great beak partly resting on its breast, it is a splendid performer in the air, soaring upwards on thermals until a mere speck in the sky. Over short distances it flies using slow wing-flapping for power, alternated with graceful glides. A bird as big as the pelican would waste precious energy becoming airborne if it did not make use of thermals. For this reason it usually feeds and nests in areas where a combination of cool water and sun-warmed ground sets up convection currents – the thermals that lift the pelican skywards. Once aloft, the bird spreads its wings and sails effortlessly over great distances in search of fresh feeding grounds. However, selection is not random and the pelican prefers to alight in areas where it can rely on rising air currents for take-off – and where fishing looks promising. At Lake Ngami in Botswana I found members of the breeding colony travelling up to 80 kilometres daily to find places that met with these two requirements.

The White Pelican nests in colonies, and at the coast shares its breeding-ground with other birds such as the Cape Cormorant. The newly-hatched chick is naked and pink, a singularly ugly and grotesque creature, like some hideous creation by Albrecht Dürer. It is fed from the parent's throat on regurgitated partly-digested fish which it must retrieve by thrusting its beak, and often its head too, deep into the adult's gullet in what appears an ordeal in the name of parenthood. The story of the pelican piercing its breast to feed its offspring is simply not true. For some strange reason this bird and the flamingo are often confused, and the blood-red fluid regurgitated by the flamingo to nourish its young gave rise to the fable of the pelican in its 'piety' which was a favourite with mediaeval churchmen as a symbol of God's mercy to man.

The pelican's most remarkable feature is its great pouched beak which is used as a net to trap fish and to hold the catch for a short time. To swallow, it raises its head and the sides of the pouch are drawn together, expelling water and retaining the fish. Pelicans favour freshwater feeding grounds and they fish together – often co-operatively – gliding majestically through the shallows until a shoal is sighted. Then, beating their wings, they form an ever-tightening circle driving the fish into the centre. In this confined area, the converging birds rhythmically dip their giant beaks in almost perfect unison, raise their heads and dip again as if at a signal.

15 White Pelicans, their breeding plumage flushed a delicate pink, feed in rich water near their nesting site on Lake Ngami in Botswana. They favour freshwater feeding grounds and they fish together – often co-operatively – gliding majestically through the shallows until a shoal is sighted.

16 A nesting colony of White Pelicans on Lake Ngami. This site has three important advantages as far as breeding birds are concerned: thermals vital for flight; a plentiful food supply close at hand, and vast open banks that isolate the colony from predators such as jackal and hyena.

16

Sacred Ibis

A sometime predator of unguarded eggs and nestlings and a devourer of carrion, the Sacred Ibis was, curiously enough, held to be divine by the Ancient Egyptians whose god of wisdom, Thoth, was represented as having the head of this bird on a human body. It seems strange that the least attractive feature of the ibis should have been held in such high esteem, naked as it is; yet, seen as a whole with its pure white plumage in strong contrast to its bare black head, the bird is strikingly beautiful. In flight it is both delicate and graceful, black-fringed wings smoothly stroking the air as it sails low across the water.

Seldom is a lone ibis encountered, for these birds are sociable by nature and choose to nest in colonies often in company with herons, egrets and cormorants. After breeding they disperse and birds ringed on the Witwatersrand have been located as far away as Zambia and even the southern part of Tanzania.

17 Black feathers splayed under stress, the pelican's powerful wings lift it from the water. This black 'lace' edging is a common feature of many larger birds and results from a concentration of the pigment melanin which strengthens those portions of the wing subject to the greatest strain and abrasion.

18 Black-fringed wings smoothly stroking the air, Sacred Ibises sail across a summer sky.

19 Gulls are usually considered sea-birds but the Grey-headed breeds on freshwater marshes and is often seen inland. Here adult birds tend their nests of twigs and grass at the water's edge while a fluffy chick scrambles back to safety after a brief excursion.

20 Mirrored reeds and infinite detail enhance a Grey-headed Gull's bright breeding plumage.

Gulls

The Kelp Gull – largest and most formidable of all South African gulls – is emphatically a sea-gull, rarely moving more than a few kilometres inland. This peripatetic bird is found in South America, New Zealand, the sub-Antarctic islands and the Australian coast.

Most gulls take a variety of food and the Kelp is no exception. A keen scavenger, it haunts rubbish dumps, canning factories and ships. Moreover it is a dedicated egg thief, and a thoughtless disturbance of a cormorant colony usually means that many eggs will be seized before the parents' return. But in nature's harsh world, the Kelp's own chicks are not immune: if they wander beyond their parents' territory they, too, may fall prey to a neighbouring pair.

Researchers have found that a gull recognises its own chick only after it is a few days old. Before that, it is possible to indiscriminately substitute one chick for another without the parents rejecting the implant. However, after the crucial period there is individual recognition and the adult will accept only its own offspring.

This ubiquitous gull enjoys mussels but, unable to break the shells with its beak, it must take the mollusc a few metres up into the air and drop it. The degree of success depends on how well the gull has learnt by experience and imitation. Immature birds drop their brittle tit-bits on the sand more often than not and have to repeat the whole process, but proficient gulls will select flat, hard expanses, such as car parks, jetties and tar roads rather than uneven rocks, and their favourite spots are littered with shattered shells. What is more, they learn to assess the optimum height from which to do the job: too high, they waste energy and take the risk that robber gulls will reach the morsel before they do; too low, and the exercise is wasted for the mussel does not break. Therefore, the 'super-gull' will only choose a large mollusc where the ratio of effort to gain is worth while, and it is not unusual to see an experienced bird carefully weighing its prospective meal in its beak before taking it up for dropping.

Young Kelp Gulls feed on regurgitated food. There is a red spot on the yellow beak of the adult and a hungry youngster instinctively pecks at this, creating a stimulus which makes the adult bring up partially-digested food. In Europe a series of fascinating experiments with allied species has shown that the young will peck at a model beak with a contrasting spot whatever the colour, though they react more readily to a yellow beak with a red spot than any other combination.

In another experiment it was established that gulls that are closely related and share common breeding sites do not hybridize because they recognise their own species visually. The deciding factor was the coloured ring that surrounds the gulls' eyes. When the characteristic colour of one species was artificially substituted by that of another, interbreeding promptly took place.

21 A Kelp Gull grasps its trophy – a Jackass Penguin's egg robbed from an unguarded nest.

22 Incorrigible opportunists, these Kelp Gulls harass immature cormorants. In their alarm the intimidated young will regurgitate food and the gulls then swoop down for an easy meal.

Albatross

Of all sea-birds, none is more spectacular than the great Wandering Albatross found only in the southern oceans. These birds – sometimes weighing as much as 9 kilograms and with a wing-span of 3,5 metres – were the subject of many fables and superstitions, and sailors believed that to kill one was to invite disaster. Indeed, it was the huge Wandering Albatross that was hung about the neck of Samuel Taylor Coleridge's Ancient Mariner as punishment after he had impetuously shot it with his crossbow.

The albatross is famed for its superb, soaring flight and the apparently effortless manner in which it hangs aloft or sweeps to and fro with long narrow wings outspread. The secret of its mastery of the air lies in its skilful use of the varying wind speeds above the oceans, coupled with the force of gravity: it will shoot down with the wind and then sweep up against it, gaining velocity downwind and lift as it is borne upwards. Skimming low over the sea, it even utilizes the updraught caused by the waves. Using these techniques, it can remain on the wing for hours, even days, but it does alight on the surface to sleep and to pick up food.

The natural food of the albatross consists of fish, squid, crustacea and even small birds, but is has also learnt to take galley refuse and trawler offal tossed overboard. Partly to enjoy this food and partly to take advantage of the air currents caused by the passage of a vessel, an albatross will follow astern for great distances; in fact it is often thought that the same bird has accompanied a ship for many days but this must be a rare happening. Usually only a few birds will be seen early in the morning but as the day wears on the number increases, suggesting that fresh contingents take over from time to time.

Six species of albatross visit the seas round southern Africa though they do not breed there. Of these, the Black-browed – smaller and more tame than the Wandering Albatross – is most numerous, particularly along the continental shelf of the west coast between the latitudes of 25°S and 28°S. Here there is an up-welling of plankton-rich water and the sea teems with life. Present throughout the year, the Black-browed Albatross is more common in winter; summer is its breeding season and it must then be away on the distant oceanic islands where it nests. Only the young immature birds are seen here all the year round.

Albatrosses, if their nesting is successful, breed only every alternate year – a result of the long, slow process of incubation and rearing. Although the young are not fed every day, they gradually grow so fat that they soon outweigh their parents and are too heavy to fly. However, as the intervals between the adults' visits increase, so the albatross chicks rely for nourishment on their own fat until eventually they become light enough to take wing. They then leave the nest and fly off to sea.

23 Outraged, a Kelp Gull reacts violently to any disturbance at the nest. Shrieking its displeasure, it dive-bombs, defecates and even flails with its powerful wings at the intruder.

For several years before it reaches maturity – and in the intervals between breeding seasons – the albatross ranges the oceans, but once it is old enough it usually returns to nest on the same small island on which it was hatched. It is difficult enough to conceive how a swallow can return year after year to the identical nesting spot, but the mind boggles at the formidable feat of the albatross in pin-pointing a minute island in the vastness of a featureless ocean.

Oystercatchers

Conspicuous on southern African shores is the Black Oystercatcher. Strangely enough, in view of its name, this bird's diet does not consist only of oysters. More usually it eats shell-fish such as mussels and limpets which it skilfully prises off rocks, as well as the burrowing white mussels for which it probes deep in sand and mud, and other marine invertebrates.

Out of the breeding season it may be seen in parties of more than 20, but at nesting time the groups separate into pairs and an entertaining and bouncy courtship follows to the accompaniment of the bird's strident, piping call. Each couple stakes out a claim to a stretch of beach and maintains this as their own property throughout the nesting season.

The nest is safely situated 40 or 50 metres above the high-tide level – though the birds sometimes miscalculate and the nest is flooded by spring tides. The nest itself is an unpretentious scrape in the sand, often surrounded by strands of dried blackish-brown kelp which help to camouflage the jet-black sitting birds.

Many of the beaches popular with picnickers and fishermen are also the Oystercatchers' nesting haunts. Although human intruders rarely molest the birds deliberately, their presence keeps them off their eggs. Without the body of the adult as a sun-shield the eggs lie fully exposed on the baking white beach sand and, left unattended for too long, they may simply cook.

To protect these birds in the Cape of Good Hope Nature Reserve, visitors will now be prohibited from the Oystercatcher's favourite nesting areas during the breeding season.

Terns

Terns are long-winged sea-birds, though more common to coastal waters than the open sea. The dozen or so species found in southern African waters range in size from the red-beaked Caspian Tern – as big as Hartlaub's Gull – to the diminutive Damara Tern. The survival of this tiny bird is now threatened – in addition to normal hazards – by that recent intruder, the beach buggy which disturbs breeding.

A great many of the terns seen in southern Africa are non-breeding migrants; the Common Tern comes from Europe, the Arctic Tern breeds in the Arctic Circle, and the two species are so alike that it is frequently impossible to differentiate between them in the field. For these birds British ornithologists have coined the useful term 'Com-ic Terns'. Most Common Terns migrate no farther than South Africa but many of the Arctic Terns move on to spend the southern summer along the edge of the Antarctic ice-pack. Their migration, almost from pole to pole, is the longest of any bird and, what is more, many of them live through continuous, or almost continuous, daylight – except on migration through the tropics.

The Common Tern has been extensively studied. It was found that not only does it breed in colonies, but within each colony there are groups of birds which regularly nest together. The social infrastructure of the Common Tern extends to include associated colonies, although terns seldom move from one colony to another. But should a bird, or more often an entire group, move from its original colony – perhaps because the site has become unsuitable – it will do so to another within its own larger circle. It also appears almost certain that each breeding group migrates and remains together in its non-breeding quarters.

Flamingoes

A mass of flamingoes, their pink and crimson plumage aglow, whether in flight or on the ground, is a magnificent sight. This beautiful colouring, for which the plumage is so much admired, derives from the small crustacea in the bird's diet which contain the pigment carotene. Before this was a recognised fact flamingoes in captivity remained inexplicably white after the first moult – the contrast being most obvious in the American form of the Greater Flamingo which is normally bright pink all over. It was only when artificial food was supplemented by live brine shrimps and similar creatures that the plumage reverted to its former familiar colour.

It seems strange that two separate species of flamingo are found in South Africa when one would surely do. The difference is basically a case of diet. The Lesser Flamingo feeds mainly on microscopic plants, while the Greater Flamingo's diet includes slightly larger organisms, more particularly tiny crustacea. Presumably, some time long ago, instead of competing for a limited food supply, flamingoes evolved in such a way that they could exploit two separate food sources – and the populations could then expand accordingly. In southern Africa the resulting species are best told apart by the colour of the beak – pale pink with a black tip in the Greater, and wholly dark red in the Lesser which, in view of its diet, is not surprisingly a smaller bird as well.

Flamingoes inhabit such salt-water estuaries and lagoons as St Lucia (where they nest), Langebaan and Walvis Bay, but the most frequent breeding place is the north-west corner of the Etosha Pan in South West Africa – and even here they do not nest every year but only after good rains.

Their nesting habits are as fascinating as their ways. They breed in colonies where there are wide expanses of shallow water unencumbered with vegetation. The nest is a cone of mud with a hollow in the top for the clutch, and is placed either on a small, low island or actually rising out of the shallows. Its height depends on the amount of mud available and, of course on the depth of the water. Flamingoes are extremely fastidious about the conditions under which they will breed and if things are not to their liking they will go no further than nest-building. However, if they are satisfied they will lay – usually one egg to a nest – and this the adult incubates, folding its long legs under its body. To feed its young the flamingo regurgitates a blood-red fluid, and in mediaeval times this remarkable food was erroneously believed to be blood.

At Etosha the nests are built at the edge of the salt pan so that they are protected from ground-dwelling predators by water on one side and by a vast stretch of mud flat on the other. Every few years, as the dry season advances, the water recedes, eventually dividing the pan into two separate and progressively shrinking pools. This presents a very real threat to the flamingo chicks: the parents with their as yet flightless young follow the margins of the retreating water, and those on the eastern part, which is liable to dry up altogether, become hopelessly marooned. Under a relentless sun, the birds now bravely turn west and set out to walk 30 or 40 kilometres across the baked mud to the distant part of the pan which still contains water. In such harsh conditions few, if any, of the chicks reach their goal and the vultures hold high carnival.

Flamingoes are filter-feeders, swinging their heads rhythmically from side to side, necks curved and the down-turned end of the beak held hockey-stick fashion. The upper mandible is ridged inside, and there is a fringe of lamellae which serves as a sieve. A feeding bird opens its beak slightly and retracts the tongue which lies in a groove in its lower jaw. In so doing it draws in water and with it the small animal and vegetable matter on which it feeds. The beak is then almost closed and the tongue thrust forward, squeezing out the water and leaving food trapped on the ridges and lamellae. What might seem a complicated process takes only a fraction of a second. These birds normally feed standing, or walking slowly through the shallows, trampling the mud to stir it up. They will also – especially in the case of the Lesser Flamingo – feed swimming, either from the surface or by up-ending like a duck.

24 On the Falkland Islands a downy Black-browed Albatross chick stares with fathomless eyes at my camera. Safe in their remote nesting places, the young birds have not yet learnt to fear man's presence.

25 Caught by a shaft of weak sunlight, a Black-browed Albatross glides to a pinnacle nest-site at West Point Island in the Falklands.

26 Stylised side-stepping, bowing and nibbling strengthen the pair-bond between courting Black-browed Albatrosses.

27 'Why the black brow?' is a question I am often asked. My friend Keith Shackleton has a simple answer: 'Because it makes symmetry and a place for the eye – the perfect design of nature!'

28 Splashed with foam from a breaking wave, Black Oystercatchers cling with tough claws and horny foot-pads to an offshore rock.

29 Terns feed by plunging and dipping into the water from a height, though they do not dive from ordinary flight but hover expectantly over the sea. Only when they have spotted their prey do they dive, and then never to any great depth.

28

30 Backs warmed by the sun, Kelp Gulls and several species of tern pattern the beach sands between bouts of fishing and foraging.

31

31 & 33 Notorious nomads, strong fliers and unpredictable visitors, flamingoes must travel great distances since they prefer arid areas with irregular rainfall. There may be hundreds, even thousands, on a stretch of water one day, then overnight they will vanish and move to another locality where they may remain for years.

32 Arise and settle, flutter and pause – restless terns at the water's edge.

32

34 A Greater Flamingo nonchalantly scratches its head as it feeds in untroubled waters.

Rivers and Vleis

Shallow water provides food for a distinctive type of bird: long-legged and long-necked and often long-beaked, too. There are the waders that stalk the shallows, beaks darting to snatch up a morsel. More patient are those, like herons, that stand on long stilt-like legs waiting for an edible tit-bit to swim into striking range, then with a jab of the bird's sharp beak the victim is caught.

Then there are those that plunge, either from a perch or from the air. To catch their prey some use their beaks, others their talons, but all are superb marksmen.

Finally there are those of the deeper water, those that dive – freshwater cormorants, for example – and those that dabble – ducks and the so-called geese. There are, in fact, no true geese in Africa. This misnomer has arisen because certain African ducks have adopted goose-like habits and characteristics to exploit habitats which would otherwise have been suited to geese had there been any here.

Egrets

Cranes and storks are frequently confused by those who know little about birds, but egrets – though zoologically a type of heron – are known to most people. Smallest, commonest and most widespread is the Cattle Egret, or Buff-backed Heron as it is known in England, which in the breeding season grows buff plumes on head, back and breast.

On the whole, egrets feed alone in shallow water but the Cattle Egret is gregarious, whole flocks seeking food on dry land. There is no altruism in the bird world: those that flock together to feed or roost are simply utilising the various advantages offered by group living. There is a price of course. The Cattle Egret's white plumage makes it a ready target for predators and it is partly for this reason that it shuns places where the grass is taller than itself and where it cannot therefore keep a wary eye open. The Cattle Egret's food is 'clumped' in certain areas and the advantage of its conspicuous plumage is that as soon as a bird comes upon an insect-rich feeding ground it is readily spotted and others descend to share the bounty. Foraging alone, a single egret would have to expend a great deal more energy finding favourable feeding areas.

As their name indicates, these egrets are generally found where there are cattle, but they will also follow various antelope, elephant, buffalo and – failing all else – sheep, pigs, donkeys and ostriches. Furthermore, they learn by imitation and having discovered, for instance, that a plough will disturb insects otherwise hidden in the ground, the birds are often seen following the ploughman.

It is common to see one or two birds perched on the back of a grazing animal, for not only does the egret feed on large blood-sucking flies that are a source of considerable irritation to the host, but it uses the moving animal to traverse areas of grass taller than itself. Now and again a bird pecks at the animal it accompanies and it is popularly thought to be removing ticks – whence the Afrikaans name *Bosluisvoël* and its English version 'Tick Bird' – but in point of fact the egret seldom eats these creatures. The egret makes further use of mammals as beaters. The moving animal flushes out insects as it grazes, which the birds following on foot feed on. In this way the egret expends approximately half the energy it would if foraging independently.

The Cattle Egret's range has extended in a remarkable manner since the beginning of the present century. Until then it was confined to the Old World from southern Europe to Asia, and south through most of Africa. By the early 1920s it had reached the Eastern Cape, then it spread westwards until it reached Cape Town where the first breeding colony was recorded in 1934. But, when compared with what had been happening elsewhere, this is insignificant for, at the turn of the century, Cattle Egrets were recorded in South America having crossed the Atlantic. It is highly unlikely that this was the first time these birds had made such a crossing. Large herbivorous animals are not indigenous to South America in significant numbers and it was only with the development of intensive cattle farming that the Cattle Egrets could establish themselves there. They were once birds solely of the marshlands where the grass was relatively short, and although still water-associated, their widening distribution can be linked to the vast meadows and cropped grasslands that are necessary to cattle farming. Indeed, with the exception of places with cold climates, wherever intensive cattle farming has been introduced in the New World, this bird has followed close behind.

Cattle Egrets breed in colonies, often with other species of egret, heron, ibis, cormorant, darter and spoonbill. Once a nesting-site has been selected, the male bird is joined by the female, who at first appears to masquerade as a male with covetous designs on his nesting ground. In anthropomorphic terms one might liken this display to a cool reappraisal of one's mate: looks, efficiency, suitability and appeal. The pair-bond is formed and nesting can begin.

Each colony has its own traditional feeding areas. However, after breeding, while several colonies may share the same roost, the individual flocks continue to visit their own particular foraging grounds.

35 Nesting Cattle Egrets proudly display their elegant plumage very similar to that of the pure white crest-feathers of related species that were all the rage at the turn of the century. So great was the demand for such feathers to grace the hats of Parisian ladies that some of these species were threatened with extinction. The fashion passed into the realms of memory but the French word *l'aigrette*, meaning plume, remains and gave the bird its English name, egret.

The top left bird's elaborate performance is instantly recognised by its mate who then allows the alighting bird to join the family at the nest. A characteristic courtship ritual exclusive to each species of egret prevents interbreeding in the large colonies.

36 High-lighted by the late afternoon sun, a pair of Cattle Egrets pause before joining the flock at a nearby roost.

38

37 Captured in fluent motion, a lone Yellow-billed Egret glides down the Okavango River in search of feeding grounds where the river spills out into its great flood-plain.

38 The Green-backed Heron's delicately striped chest mirrors the shape of the trailing leaves of reeds in its riverside habitat.

39 Its posture closely resembling the stark outlines of the dead branches of its breeding site, this Black-headed Heron was nesting strangely alone. More usually, communities of these birds breed in mixed heronries.

40 The Purple Heron blends perfectly with its surroundings, particularly when it stands with head, neck and beak stretched upwards as it does when alarmed. It is a determined skulker and spends much of its time in reed-beds only occasionally coming into the open. In this case the correlation between plumage and habitat is undeniable, particularly in a bird that depends on stealth to find its food. Here camouflage is part of the bird's adaptation as an effective hunter in very specialised surroundings.

40

41 Poised at nest's edge like some great winged ballet dancer the spoonbill prepares to tend its chick, a surprisingly minute creature barely visible above the sides of the nest.

42 As a party of spoonbills stalks off in one direction, a White-faced Duck comes in to land. Like the flamingo, the spoonbill feeds by sweeping its beak back and forth in the water. The inner surface of the spatulate area is extremely sensitive to touch so that the bird instantly traps tiny waterborne organisms and even small fish. It also probes the mud, clappering its jaws in a manner peculiar to its kind.

44

43-44 Spoonbills rise in an exquisite aerial pyramid from an exposed river-bank where they were resting in the heat of the day. The Okavango flood-plain is a favourite haunt of freshwater birds, including the spoonbill, which feed on the rich concentrations of waterlife that collect in the endless small shallow ponds at the end of winter before the rains come.

45 Arrogant sentinels on a burnt-out tree, White-bellied Storks gaze out over the scorched veld. Known as avid fire-followers, storks feed on the myriads of trapped insects and the charred remains of those not so lucky to escape.

46 Amid shimmering heat and blue smoke from a veld fire, White Storks search for insects flushed out by the flames.

47 Looking like some monstrous prehistoric bird, the Wood Stork comes in to land.

48 As dusk approaches, scores of Openbills swoop down to roost on a bank on the Zambezi River. The open space in the centre of the bird's bill helps it handle the slippery freshwater clams that this bird relishes.

48

Herons

There are few guarantees in nature's world and, to survive, each bird must maximize its chances of successful breeding. The Purple Heron is a case in point. Firstly, the size of the clutch is determined by the number of young the adults can rear to fledgling stage – and this itself is directly linked to various factors, perhaps the most important being food supply. The Purple Heron's normal clutch is three, but in a good year the female may lay four eggs and all will probably reach fledgling stage. In leaner times the clutch may be smaller and, with such birds as the flamingo, unsatisfactory conditions will inhibit laying altogether.

Another gamble in the game of survival is that the eggs are always laid in sequence with, in the case of the heron, something like six to eight days' difference in age between the first and the last. By the time the youngest chick hatches its older siblings are already far stronger and wiser in the ways of their world. When the parent brings food back to the nest the older birds are first to get it – the youngest must hopefully wait its turn or compete in an unequal struggle. If food is plentiful then it, too, will eventually get its share and stand a good chance of reaching fledgling stage. On the other hand, if food is scarce, the bird is doomed: too young and weak to successfully compete with the rest of the brood it simply starves to death. But beware a value judgement; the weakest may be lost but those that survive will perpetuate the species.

The efficiency of the system can be gauged by imagining a situation in which all the eggs in a clutch were hatched together. It would mean a brood of equally competitive chicks which would each take an equal share of a food supply limited by what the adult can find and carry. None of the chicks would be strong and well-nourished, the parent would be exhausted by the effort, with the end result that parent and offspring would be imperilled. What is more, as far as the parent is concerned, to ensure a few healthy fledglings is paramount, and that one or two chicks may have to be sacrificed is a small price to pay for survival.

Storks

The White-bellied, or Abdim's, is the smallest stork found in southern Africa.

It breeds in tropical North Africa, migrating south during the southern summer. Great flocks pass over the Congo Forests, probably at a great height, but small parties are known to alight occasionally in clearings. They move constantly between the northern and southern tropical belts according to the wet seasons when the combination of heat and rain ensures plentiful insects. By no means confined by its feeding habits to watery places, the White-bellied Stork likes to hunt on cultivated land and, as it devours great numbers of locusts during their swarming phase, it is welcomed by farmers. Nevertheless, persistent use of insecticides threatens these birds which eat locusts indiscriminately, whether poisoned or not.

The White Stork is a European migrant with a small breeding colony in the southern Cape. Many years ago some of the visiting birds were incapacitated and could not make the return trip to Europe. It would appear that their descendants established a colony near Bredasdorp where they are actively encouraged by farmers who erect wagon-wheels on posts as nesting platforms, and even go so far as to stabilize the nests with wire. This stork is also the 'baby stork' of fairy tales, and this might well have influenced the special treatment it receives from the local population.

The Wood Stork has a yellow, slightly curved beak like that of an ibis, but it is neither a wood-dweller nor an ibis, but a species of stork. Small flocks migrate from tropical Africa, a few reaching as far south as the Cape, but they breed in Zululand where the birds build nests of sticks high in tall trees. Their table manners are out of the ordinary, in that they sometimes dine in water deep enough to immerse the entire head.

Marabou Storks

Huge in size and repulsive to look at, the Marabou Stork is a species closely related to the Indian Adjutant which Rudyard Kipling, in his *Jungle Books*, described as 'a ruffianly brute'. At the base of its neck is an ugly bare pouch which may be inflated and is directly connected with the left nostril so that it acts as a resonator for the bird's guttural croak. But its most remarkable feature is its enormous beak which has been aptly likened to a pick-axe. The Marabou flies with its neck bent into a flattened S to accommodate its heavy beak which then rests on the shoulders.

Besides sometimes catching fish and frogs in shallow water, the Marabou has another feeding habit more in keeping with its disreputable appearance – that of joining vultures at a carcase or a slaughter-house. In Uganda, at least, almost all its food is carrion and offal. This is probably the reason why the head and neck of the Marabou, like those of the vulture, are almost bare of feathers, since this nakedness reduces the possibility of contamination from putrefying flesh. Because of its powerful bill, vultures pay it due respect, and when the two are rivals, the Marabou is master. In search of carrion it cruises at a great height, scanning the country below for signs of dead animals. Once its sharp eyes pick out a likely meal it descends slowly, sweeping the sky in broad circles; then it lowers its legs, points its beak down, and swiftly drops. On the ground it stalks across the veld, hideous head hunched between its shoulders and when it has eaten its fill, flaps up into a tree to rest.

The Marabou sometimes breeds in cliffs – there is a famous colony at the Kalambo Falls in north-eastern Zambia – but it is more usual for communities to nest in a large tree, such as the baobab. A great many assemble to breed in the swamp fig thickets of the Okavango.

49

Bald Ibis

The Bald Ibis is a peculiar-looking bird and a species unique to South Africa. Its only close relative, the Hermit Ibis, is on the verge of extinction and is quite as odd-looking. At one time, not long ago, it was feared that the Bald Ibis, too, was endangered. However, a survey in the Transvaal, Natal and the Orange Free State revealed a number of hitherto unknown breeding colonies and it appears that for the moment the species is safe. Nevertheless the range has contracted quite considerably over the last 200 years. As late as 1906 one was taken at Milnerton, near Cape Town, but today it is virtually extinct south and west of Lesotho and East Griqualand. It is not certain why this is so, but a major factor, no doubt, has been human persecution for the bird is said to make excellent eating.

It is less dependent on water than the other ibises, feeding to a large extent in open grassland where it probes the ground for the grubs and worms that make up much of its diet. Insects such as grasshoppers, beetles and caterpillars are captured above ground and it is not averse to eating carrion. Amazingly enough, its already varied diet sometimes includes buttons, presumably mistaken for beetles! Small parties of the birds are most likely to be spotted foraging in the immediate vicinity of their nesting or roosting place, and this voluntary restriction in movement may account for the belief in their rarity.

The Bald Ibis is a cliff-nester and the colony is conspicuous from afar by the 'white-washing' of droppings that streak the cliff-face. Both parents take turns at incubating the clutch, and when changing over go through an exaggerated display accompanied by resounding calls in which neighbouring birds may join.

49 Stilt-like legs exaggerated by reflection, Saddlebills stare at the camera. These birds are among a host of species that profit from the rain-water pans that dot tropical southern Africa after the wet season. Once the rains are over, these pans gradually evaporate, the waterlife being forced into an ever-smaller habitat and, as far as feeding birds are concerned, an ever-richer one. Mammals that come down to drink litter the bank with manure which the following rainy season is submerged to provide a nutrient-rich medium for a new flush of waterlife.

50 Alighting on a swamp fig thicket a Marabou spreads its wings in a gesture of greeting while the other bird assumes a submissive downward pose.

51

51 A fisherman's simple craft provides the clue to the Marabou's presence here. Fishing villages throughout Africa draw these lazy birds with the promise of an easy meal from the offal discarded after the catch is gutted.

52 In keeping with its ugly face and repulsive habits, the Marabou's legs gleam white with faeces. There were two schools of thought on why this bird defecates on its legs: it was originally suggested that the strongly alkaline waste-matter acted as a disinfectant on that part of the bird's body most likely to be tainted with carrion in the course of its gastronomic adventures, but modern research has proved that it cools the creature's legs and so assists with thermo-regulation.

52

53

53 A Bald Ibis safe in its mountain refuge 20 metres above a broad, swiftly-flowing stream. This colony, unknown until recently, is the roosting-place of 60 or more youngsters in addition to the 15 or 20 pairs that make it their breeding site.

54 Crouched motionless at the water's edge a Squacco Heron waits for a small fish, tadpole or water-beetle to come into beak-range. It is a successful bird of compromise. During the day it feeds alone and its brown and striped plumage proves admirable camouflage among the waterplants and sedges. However, at night it roosts in flocks and must congregate quickly. Therefore on the wing it appears a conspicuous white which helps it find its fellows as dusk approaches.

55 Like the work of some modern abstract artist, the Crowned Crane's face and magnificent headdress fill the picture.

54

56 Protected by superstition in the Transkei, the Crowned Cranes there are totally unafraid of humans. Earlier in the day I encountered them wandering freely among the village huts in the background.

Cranes

South Africa's national bird, the Blue or Stanley Crane, is the smallest of the African cranes and is less closely attached to water than its fellows, but its ancestry is obvious in that it roosts when possible standing in water. The habit no doubt evolved as a defence mechanism but, for the birds, it is instinctive rather than reasoned. Two Blue Cranes which a friend of mine kept as pets always roosted in the water of a small goldfish pool although it provided no more protection from predators than roosting on the ground.

The long graceful plumes which trail behind the bird when it walks are the secondary flight feathers of the wing and not the tail feathers as is commonly thought. Like all members of the crane family, the Blue Crane has an elaborate courting ritual and these delicate wing plumes play an important visual role in the dance.

Cranes are omnivorous and this species makes itself particularly unpopular in some areas by scouring newly-planted fields for grain. However, locusts and other large insects, lizards and frogs also form part of its diet, and help offset the negative aspects of its feeding patterns.

Among many flocking birds, including the Wattled Crane, a combination of black and white plumage acts as a social signal and actually promotes flocking behaviour. The wattles from which this species gets its name are used in courtship and also help dissipate heat from the bird's body.

Cranes are a relatively small family which was once much more abundant. That they are evolutionarily on the downgrade is in part response to the gradual shrinking over many millennia of the wetlands of the world. The three species found in South Africa are very different in appearance, and to some extent in habits.

Perhaps most decorative of the African crane species is the Crowned which is also the most easily identified – that is, if you see it, for although widely distributed over southern Africa its preference for swampy habitats restricts it to certain very limited areas. It is surprising that so large and strikingly attractive a bird – and one by no means inedible – should survive in the protein-hungry Transkei where far smaller birds are relentlessly hunted. Fortunately it is protected by taboo, the black peoples regarding it with great superstition which inhibits them from killing it.

The Crowned Crane's loud, nasal voice – and the two-syllabled call from which its vernacular names 'Mahem' and 'Ongwan' come – serves to keep together a flock that may number as many as 300. All cranes perform quaint courtship dances and this one is no exception – gracefully hopping and jumping about with wings partly spread. At times this rapturous state will affect a flock simultaneously and the multiple performance makes a glorious spectacle. However, more often only a pair is involved for this species is believed to mate for life.

57 A flight of Crowned Cranes returns to roost on a small island at the mouth of the Nxaxo River on the Transkei coast.

58 Eyes glistening in the light of my flash, roosting Crowned Cranes stand like palace guards in full dress regalia. At night small parties assemble here until eventually some 200 birds share the sanctuary.

59 Animals stopped mid-drink to stare at this noisy mob of Blue Cranes whose distinctive bugling cry rang out over the plains as they approached. Only recently have Blue Cranes appeared in significant numbers at the edge of the Etosha Pan in South West Africa, and they have begun to breed here, too.

60 Highly-prized by zoos all over the world, the Wattled Crane is a magnificent creature. In the rain puddles of tropical Africa it feeds on the submerged roots and corms of plants which it digs up with its long shovel-like beak.

61 Only its alert eye belies the peaceful symmetry of a resting Yellowbill. Beak tucked beneath its feathers, it conserves heat on the chilly water by hiding naked areas in the warmth of its plumage.

60

Ducks

Ducks and so-called geese are widespread throughout Africa and the species are broadly divisible into two: tropical and non-tropical. When compared with their northern hemisphere counterparts they are a dull lot, none of the southern species sharing, say, the male Mallard's superb colouring. The northern male's finery is, in part, a solution to a situation where in the three short months of summer the ducks migrate to the far northern areas and must nest, lay, incubate, rear and fledge their young within this brief period. There is no time for prolonged courtship displays if the full breeding cycle is to be encompassed within the limited time-span and to speed the proceedings the male duck sports his beautiful plumage to quickly woo and win a mate. That his colouring makes him conspicuous to predators is a risk he must take.

In the southern hemisphere food is not as concentrated in time and space as in the north, but there is a long warm summer during which to breed. What is more, the southern species do not migrate. Courtship is more protracted and the male depends as much on long elaborate displays as on his rather dowdy looks. With time on his side, it is not necessary for him to risk losing his camouflage to win a bride.

Apart from a few specialists such as the Black Duck, waterfowl generally prefer shallow water to deep, and temporary pools to permanent lakes. As the rainy season passes many of these birds must move long distances to find water again. Research based on the recovery of ringed birds has revealed that as the dry winter approaches, some of the waterfowl of the Transvaal, Zambia and the Caprivi move north and across the Equator to exploit the tropical flood-plains of the Sudan.

Shallow waters, fresh and salt, are limited in the semi-arid areas that make up much of southern Africa. Here the seasonal drying-up of rivers, vleis and pans plays an important part in maintaining a food chain that ensures waterbirds a rich source of food the following season. As the dry season progresses game and livestock follow the receding water's edge and leave in their paths manure which the next season's rains convert into a nutrient-rich environment for the waterlife on which so many birds depend. But, as if the unreliability and erratic distribution of temporary waters in southern Africa were not hazard enough, man poses a further threat. Vast industrial developments are destroying the waterfowl's natural habitat. Drainage for agriculture all too often results in the destruction

62 A mother White-faced Duck shepherds her youthful brood over a marshy flood-plain.

of the natural 'sponge' that holds the water, and can turn a grassy vlei into a barren waste scarred by eroded watercourses which rapidly carry away the rain. Additionally, the deepening of dams simply means the loss of potential feeding grounds.

The duck which you are most likely to see in South Africa is the Yellowbill which, bill-colour apart, looks like the female Mallard of the northern hemisphere. In fact, the Mallard and the Yellowbill occupy the same niche in the order of things in the bird world: one in Africa and the other in Europe and North America. This resemblance between the species poses a potential threat. Pet Mallards kept by bird-lovers in southern Africa escape and out in the wild the male's elegant plumage proves irresistible to the female Yellowbill – rather like seduction of the simple village maiden by the city slicker. As has already happened in New Zealand where the situation was similar, the offspring of this pair is superior to both parents and gradually begins to dominate the aquatic habitat on which the local species depends. The danger lies in that the indigenous species, in this case the Yellowbill, may eventually be replaced by a new breed, the old order dying out.

Rape is generally attributed to man, but in the avian world the duck too shares this dubious distinction. Important to the concept of rape is the penis, and the duck together with the ostrich and one or two other birds, is so equipped. In the normal course of events at the outset of the breeding season the Yellowbill finds a mate and courtship follows in a gentlemanly fashion. However, it is not unusual for the female Yellowbill to be raped by several drakes in succession if for any reason her first clutch has been lost. Driven by her procreative instinct she will dispense with the niceties of courtship with various males to find the most suitable, and instead will fly up into the air to actively solicit rape. There is ready response, and after successive drakes have copulated with her she will lay a new clutch and hope that it will succeed in the time left for breeding. Moreover, in the Yellowbill's chauvinist world the male role is limited purely to the sexual and the drakes are of no interest to her after mating. She alone will incubate her eggs and care for the ducklings.

At laying time the breast feathers of female dabbling ducks loosen and they pluck these to line their nests. Normally this is done only once the last egg is laid, and the down serves to insulate the clutch – particularly when the female leaves it twice a day to feed. For an hour and a half at dawn and dusk she covers the eggs and flies off. The speckled feathers not only keep them warm but also serve as a form of camouflage. If, however, a predator should destroy this first clutch she has insufficient down to line her next nest properly and this adds to the vulnerability of a second brood.

The Yellowbill is not a ready traveller and it is rare indeed to find a bird more than 300 kilometres from the place where it was originally ringed. The population in one area fluctuates quite considerably according to the food resources, and in good years large numbers will settle to breed if there is a rich concentration of waterplants, yet ignore the place in poorer times.

The Knob-billed Duck – particularly the male – is sometimes erroneously called a goose. This is not surprising in view of its large size and the fact that its beak has become deeper as an adaptation to stripping seed-heads off grass. However, the big fleshy knob that graces the top of the drake's beak is without doubt its most striking feature. This bulge is the avian equivalent of a male secondary sexual characteristic and it is more prominent during the breeding season when it swells in size according to the social status and dominance of the drake. Young and inexperienced males sport modest knobs, while the older and more aggressively successful are better endowed. Apart from attracting females during the courtship period, the knob is also a signal to other males of the drake's social position. Whereas there is a correlation between the size of the knob and dominance, shape serves a completely different purpose: it assists in individual recognition, its configuration varies accordingly, and each knob is distinctive.

The Knob-billed Duck is polygynous, a successful drake offering his mates a territory rich in food, a suitable nesting hole near by (preferably in the bole of a tree), and his guaranteed protection from the aggressive behaviour of other males. He may take his wives successively, leaving each one once nesting is under way, or he may preside over a harem.

His courtship is slow and deliberate since he stages most of the performance in the trees. Such a precarious platform demands a laterally orientated display and he hops along the branches, his specially adapted claws helping him balance all the while. Having staked his territory and won his mates, the Knob-billed cannot afford to cease his vigilance. Since one drake takes several females, there are always a number of young unattached males skulking about in the hope of stealing one or more of his 'wives'. Indeed, if the harem becomes too large to manage, the younger drakes, skilled rapists as they are, often succeed in forcing their favours on some of the females and may even challenge the master by enticing away a few of his mates. With a premium on breeding-females there is a great deal of fighting among males for dominance and in defence of hard-won territory. Little real damage is done, but much dramatic wing-beating and tilting takes place among males in the trees. With much the same purpose as the jousting tournaments of old, competitors attempt to knock one another from their perches, and the victor's prize is prestige.

Similar in size and shape to the Yellowbill is the Black Duck, but it is a bird of very different habits. It does not gather in flocks and normally only when accompanied by a string of ducklings will more than a single pair be seen. Whereas the Yellowbill is a bird of vleis and flooded areas, of sewage farms and dams, the Black Duck is a river bird.

Each pair zealously defends its own stretch of river; indeed the best chance of seeing three or four together is when such territorial disputes are in progress. The availability of food

63 The white flash from which this bird gets its name clearly visible, a White-backed Duck punches at the water with its feet to become airborne.

plays an important role in determining the length of river one pair will appropriate. This species will sometimes feed out of water and, in the Cape, has developed a partiality for acorns which provide a filling meal for little effort. When they are freely available the duck quickly fills its crop and then spends much of the rest of the day loafing. Hidden by dappled waters and its black and white cryptic colouring, the Black Duck generally keeps well out of sight, hiding in the shadow of overgrown banks and rarely venturing out mid-stream.

64 An impala watches impassively as a flock of Red-bill Teal swoop over a grassy vlei. Intrepid travellers, birds ringed in South Africa have been found thousands of kilometres away.

65 On a partially submerged island White-faced Duck keep a wary look-out in the company of a lone spoonbill.

66 Knob-billed Ducks settle against a backdrop softened by dusk's gentle light. Only moments before they had come whiffling down and then dropped with a loud plop on the surface.

66

67 A bird to be reckoned with, this male Knob-billed Duck sports his symbol of dominance and social status – the large fleshy knob from which this species derives its name. It is only during the breeding season that the knob swells to these proportions, at other times of the year it is far less conspicuous.

68 At least 11 species of birds, plus a gallery of buck, gather to feed at a pan on the Chobe River flood-plain. A splendid habitat, the waters provide food for a wide variety of birds. Pelicans dip their capacious bagged beaks in deeper water for fish and frogs, ducks rest up on a protected sand spit, Openbill Storks search the shallows for freshwater clams, and skimmers reap the surface.

68

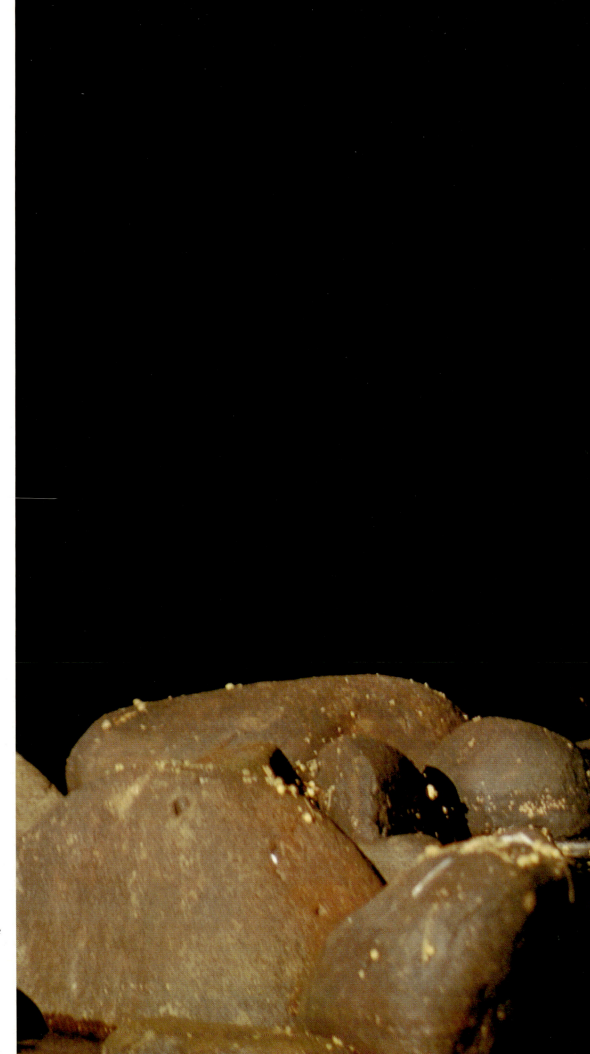

69 Specks of forest-blossom frost the river habitat of a pair of Black Ducks.

70 Perhaps the most beautiful of all southern African waterfowl is the Pygmy Goose. Here on the Okavango flood-plain when danger approached they slipped under lily pads leaving only their bill-tips above water.

71 Powerful wingbeats actually squeak with effort as Spurwing Geese fly above a reed-fringed bank on the Zambezi River. Keeping them company, an Openbill soars above.

Pygmy Goose

Most lovely of all southern African waterfowl is the Pygmy Goose. The beauty of its colouring might be thought by those who have never seen this so-called goose in its natural haunts, to make it conspicuous, but this is not the case. It chooses tranquil lagoons and lily-studded backwaters where, among the green and brown leaves and white flowers of the water-lilies, the little goose blends into the background and is very difficult to spot. When it does take off, it flies low over the water for no great distance to settle again and merge into the vegetation. It is usually found in pairs or small parties, rarely in flocks.

A tropical species very occasionally found south of Rhodesia and Natal, it makes its headquarters on the lagoons of the Okavango and the wide flood-plains of Zambia.

The Pygmy 'Goose' derives its name from its rather deep bill, adapted to deal with water-lily seeds which form its staple diet and which it supplements with other seeds, buds and aquatic insects. Its short legs – a most un-gooselike feature – are ill-suited to walking and it dives only when pressed. True geese mate for life, are exclusively ground-nesters and never perch on trees. In contrast, African 'geese' find new mates each year, use old nests, often well off the ground, and perch freely on trees with their specially adapted feet.

Spurwing Geese

Largest of the southern African waterfowl is the Spurwing Goose which gets its name from the powerful 2,5-centimetre spur on the angle of the wing, with which it can inflict severe wounds on marauding predators and rivals. Spurwings are widely distributed in Africa and move about a good deal, usually avoiding dry areas. Often they seek a safe place in which to moult, for without their flight feathers – which are shed all at once – they are unable to fly and are easy victims of predators.

In developed areas the Spurwing Goose has a habit of foraging on lucerne and young grain, and the effect of a gaggle of these big birds – a male may weigh as much as 9 kilograms – on a field of sprouting corn may well be imagined. It is no wonder that farmers dislike them for, in addition to devouring the young plants, their indiscriminate trampling causes considerable damage. Altogether formidable, in captivity it has been known to drive away cranes and to kill birds as large as the Black Swan.

72 Unusual to be out in the open during daylight, this Water Dikkop put its head down and dashed for cover as soon as it saw me. This species is generally unwilling to take to the wing and in fact spends most of the day squatting on the ground under a bush. During the crepuscular hours it ventures out to feed, its large, white-rimmed eyes well-adapted to finding food in the dim light.

73 Barely depressing the lily pads, an African Jacana trots on its large splayed feet which effectively distribute its weight over a wide area in an excellent adaptation to running over a yielding mass of waterplants.

72

Jacanas

As its common name 'Lily-trotter' indicates, the jacana (correctly pronounced *hasana*) is highly specialized for life on floating vegetation, and despite its extraordinarily long toes it has a certain grace. The large splayed feet which effectively distribute the bird's weight over a wide area are excellently adapted to running over a yielding mass of waterplants. The jacana is a tropical bird whose distribution is limited by the availability of suitable waterplants.

Its essential dependence on water vegetation is reflected in its nesting habits. On some sheltered backwater, using a platform of emergent vegetation as a base, it builds a small floating nest by drawing plants together. Chicks hatched on this precarious structure must, perforce, be precocious to survive and immediately take to water and walk freely on the vegetation. The eggs are distinctive, being remarkably glossy, pear-shaped and profusely marked with lines and scrolls of black on a yellowish ground.

Polygyny is not uncommon among birds but polyandry is rare indeed. By its very nature it can only take place in areas where food is abundant and the jacana, living as it does in the tropical marshlands of southern Africa, is ideally placed for this activity. Here the female takes her mates one at a time and then leaves them to incubate and rear the nestlings while she flies off to find her next suitor and breed again. The fathers appear to adapt well to this apparent reversal of the traditional male/female roles and have been known to carry the chicks under their wings to safety when a predator is about.

Crakes

A very different bird is the shy Black Crake which seldom leaves the reed-beds in which it lives though, when all is quiet, it may venture a short way in search of food – chiefly small aquatic animals – only to dash back to cover at the first alarm. It is adapted to this sort of existence, for its laterally compressed body slips easily through dense vegetation and reeds. The Black Crake is more often heard than seen: its high-pitched clucking, which often ends in a deep croak, is instantly recognizable. Long toes help it to swim effectively, but more often the Crake walks or climbs on half-submerged waterplants, jerking its tail at each step. Like the duck, the Black Crake sheds all its flight feathers simultaneously at moulting time and is therefore temporarily flightless. Needless to say it keeps an even lower profile then, for it is at its most vulnerable.

At times the Crake is an exponent of polygamy – indeed several females may assist with the incubating and feeding of the

74 The glint of its eye mirrored below, an African Jacana withdraws to a secluded spot.

75 Legs trailing and toes curled, an African Jacana flies jerkily over a tangled reed-bed.

75

chicks and an earlier brood may even help with the feeding of new additions. It is unusual among birds to find the equivalent of an extended family co-operating with one another for a common cause – the next generation.

With the rails, the crakes form a widespread and ancient family, and although they do not generally travel a great deal they are able to traverse the oceans. Almost every year one or two rails find their way to the south-west Cape having been blown across the Atlantic by westerly winds, while many more turn up annually on Tristan da Cunha. Over the centuries birds of this family have successfully colonized a number of oceanic islands where, in the absence of predators, they had no need to fly and as a result eventually became flightless. Unfortunately, with the intrusion of man and his attendant cats, rats and pigs into their hitherto secure refuges, all too many of these vulnerable birds have become extinct.

76 The Lesser Jacana resembles exactly the African Jacana's precocious chick. Evolved from a common ancestor, at some stage the Lesser discovered that it could survive perfectly well without growing any bigger. The newly-hatched African Jacana is at once at home moving about its precarious habitat and the Lesser Jacana's smaller size is an obvious evolutionary conclusion.

77 The shy Black Crake seldom leaves the reed-beds in which it lives, though when all is quiet it may venture a short way in search of food – chiefly small aquatic animals – only to dash back to cover at the first alarm.

African Skimmer

One of the most extraordinary birds is the skimmer, and its peculiarity is its beak. Not only does the lower mandible project far beyond the upper but the entire beak is compressed from side to side so that at the tip it resembles a paper-knife. There is sound reason for this: at dawn and dusk the skimmer feeds on the wing, flying low over the water in a leisurely manner, its lower mandible skimming the surface. As soon as the sensitive beak touches something edible it triggers an automatic reflex. Instantly, the beak snaps and the small fish or aquatic creature is firmly clamped in the upper part of the beak before being swallowed.

The African Skimmer is a long-winged tropical species of the great rivers and lakes, its distribution reaching as far south as St Lucia. Its movements are coupled to changing water levels, for as the floods subside so do the skimmers appear and prepare to nest on the emerging banks, laying their eggs in shallow scrapes in the sand. If a predator approaches, the parent skimmer makes a frantic attempt to distract it, flopping to the ground a short distance from the nest, wings beating helplessly, and the whole demonstration punctuated by sharp yapping cries.

78 Damp and exhausted, a freshly-hatched African Skimmer joins its slightly older and already fluffy sibling. The lighter tip on the newborn chick's beak marks the so-called 'egg tooth', a small hardened protruberance with which it breaks out of its confining shell. Within a day or two this 'tooth' will drop off. Eggs and chicks share the same blotch patterning against a sandy ground colour that will help camouflage them in their nest surroundings when most vulnerable.

79 Besides its unusual beak, the Skimmer has evolved remarkable bifocal vision to cope with its manner of feeding: it is able to look ahead to see where it is flying while simultaneously scanning the water below for a likely meal.

78

80 The Cape Wagtail is a favourite with all. It is as much at home pecking scraps off doorsteps as haunting desolate beaches, pursuing a fugitive grasshopper or perched on a rock in midstream. Its name comes from the way it wags its tail up and down when standing still. This is not merely a charming idiosyncrasy; the tail's prime function is to act as a rudder as the bird twists and turns after elusive insects, and to disturb them as it walks along the ground.

Kingfisher

Of all African kingfishers the most beautiful is the brilliantly-coloured and aptly named Malachite Kingfisher. This tiny, agile bird is widely distributed throughout southern Africa on streams, lakes and even small pools where it stands out like a small blue jewel in the surrounding vegetation. To feed, it perches close to the water, often on a reed stem, from which it will dive for small fish, tadpoles, beetles and other insects. On the wing it is a glorious sight, moving with lightning rapidity, darting off when disturbed and skimming over the water surface.

The Malachite Kingfisher nests in burrows which it excavates in the vertical bank of a stream or river. The tunnel, up to a metre in length, may be used for two or more consecutive seasons, and opens up into a chamber where the glossy white eggs are laid. The litter of fishbones and insect remains found on the floor of the chamber were once believed to constitute the kingfisher's nest and the British Museum was prepared to pay the handsome reward of £100 for an intact specimen! Actually these birds do not build nests but lay their eggs on the bare earth. The debris which surrounds them is merely the regurgitated remains of indigestible food. Most birds remove faeces from the nest; however, in the case of burrow-nesting species this is not so easily done and represents a waste of precious energy in a bird that must work hard to find its food. The kingfisher's chicks cope with this by defecating in particular spots in the burrow so that the nest is not itself fouled but, by the time they are old enough to emerge from the tunnel, it is – needless to say – evil-smelling.

The largest species of this bird is the Giant Kingfisher, noted particularly for its sexual dimorphism in plumage: in the male the breast is chestnut and the belly spotted in white and black, while in the female the colours are reversed. The Giant Kingfisher is a riverine bird which perches on low branches or rocks to seek its prey – crabs for the most part – and then plunges in. It then retires to its perch with its victim which is quickly beaten and stunned before being swallowed. River crabs, a particular delicacy, the kingfisher prepares by neatly nipping off the legs before making its meal. Small piles of crab legs found along many rivers and streams are evidence of this eating habit.

The Giant Kingfisher, like the Malachite, breeds in a tunnel in a sandbank. Each pair presides over a stretch of river from which the birds noisily drive out rivals, their loud and ringing cry often serving to make their presence known when they themselves are otherwise hidden by vegetation.

81 Like a priceless jewel set in a matrix of clay, a Malachite Kingfisher excavates its nesting-burrow. Shovelling feet toss out loosened debris.

82 The bigger you are the deeper you dive – or so I thought until I experimented with this Giant Kingfisher. Normally this bird plunges deep to fish, but when tempted by a surface morsel, it could not resist. Spread wings broke its fall and it proved a far more versatile hunter than had previously been supposed.

82

83 In the privacy of a reed-bed, a Malachite Kingfisher contemplates the deepening gloom.

84 A Malachite Kingfisher drip-dries on a reed-stem. Covered in dust from his home-building in a nearby bank, he dips in the river to wash and then with a shake of his feathers, dries on his mud-spattered, much-used perch.

Fish Eagles

The Fish Eagle is a splendid creature, its imposing appearance and challenging call symbolic of the African wetlands. Not that it is confined to the wilderness: indeed it sometimes makes its home close to large cities.

The expressive term 'raptor' fits this bird well for it swoops down to pluck fish from the water with its fierce talons. I recall once, on a windy day, marvelling as a Fish Eagle swept down again and again in a magnificent stoop to snatch fish carried along by the wash. Several times, as I sat watching, my attention was caught by a cormorant that had followed a fish towards the shore, but, on surfacing, the bird suddenly made off into the lake as fast as it could go. Next moment, the eagle flashed down and seized the fish but the cormorant was obviously taking no chances that the indisputably superior bird might suddenly decide on a change of diet!

This is not the Fish Eagle's only way of hunting. In the dry season, when the fish are crowded together in shallow water, it may alight and hunt on foot, and will make a meal of any stranded fish it may chance upon. Chicks in the nest are another delicacy. A few years ago, at Rondevlei Bird Sanctuary near Cape Town, a Fish Eagle took up its perch each day on a water-tower overlooking a heronry. Its patience was never rewarded for the birds were only nest-building, but so sinister was its vigilant presence that it inhibited laying and the whole colony was abandoned for that season.

It is likely, however, that this particular eagle was a youngster, for immature birds prefer to feed off nestlings and carrion rather than take the risks of hunting in water. A great many inexperienced Fish Eagles do not survive their attempts to emulate the adults' hunting methods. This species either flies at great speed along the water and snatches fish from near the surface, or – more dangerous – dives to capture its victim. The photographic sequence clearly shows how the bird may plunge almost completely into the water to reach its prey. If it does not succeed on its first try, it will dive again, each time becoming more water-logged. Younger and less proficient birds often find themselves too wet and weak from repeated efforts to lift themselves from the water and occasionally drown or are snapped up by cruising crocodiles.

Sometimes Fish Eagles bully herons into disgorging their prey. I have seen this happen only twice myself, and each time – unfortunately for the eagle – it had chosen the biggest South African heron – the Goliath. The heron crouched down with its dagger-like beak thrust upwards and the eagle, after one or two abortive stoops, gave up and went in search of an easier meal.

85 Proud symbol of the African wetlands, the majestic Fish Eagle soars aloft, its serrated black wing-tips silhouetted against the sky.

86 Erect and masterful, this Fish Eagle surveys its domain with an arrogant eye.

87

88

87 Claws extended, a Fish Eagle about to snatch a fish from the river surface.

88 Later in the day it flew down once more in a magnificent stoop to catch a fish shown here just breaking the surface of the water.

89 Wet but triumphant, this Fish Eagle proved himself a master of the deep-diving hunting method. On his first attempt he plunged down, immersing himself almost completely, skilfully took his prey and then, with powerful strokes of his wings, drew himself clear of the water. Only the most proficient adult birds survive to perfect this method. Younger birds follow one unsuccessul dive with another, until waterlogged, and occasionally have been known to drown in the effort.

Marsh Harrier

Harriers are long-winged, long-tailed birds of prey which hunt by flying low over the ground and pouncing on frogs, lizards and small birds and mammals. The African Marsh Harrier, as its name indicates, is an inhabitant of swampy ground though it will sometimes forage in dry areas provided there is water near by.

As is the case with most birds of prey, the female is larger than the male, and her three or four eggs are laid in a reed-and-stick nest built low among the rushes. During incubation – for which the female is responsible – and while the chicks are in the nest, the male provides the food. Sometimes he drops it down to her but more often she flies up to him and he passes it to her in mid-air – what appear from the ground to be clumsy movements are, in fact, a series of extremely dextrous transfer manoeuvres. Harriers also have a curious method of capturing their prey: the bird checks in flight and falls down suddenly as if shot. But it does not exclusively catch what it eats, for it will devour carrion, too, if this is available.

90 Perfectly blended with the tawny winter grass, a Marsh Harrier hangs momentarily in the breeze before pouncing.

The Veld

The grasslands of southern Africa stretch over the vast central plateau. From the lush, well-watered eastern escarpment the grass gradually becomes sparser as one travels west and rainfall diminishes. These are the savannah grasslands, an area that once teemed with game, but now farms and ranches have dramatically altered much of it, at the same time tipping the ecological balance in favour of some bird species and against others. For grain-eaters like the quelea farmers' fields provide a new, food-rich habitat and they thrive and increase. Others, like the Cape Vulture, find that factors crucial to their continued existence have been altered, placing them in jeopardy.

Ostrich

Throughout the length and breadth of this vast open veld ranges the largest of living birds, the ostrich. Some consider it evidence of the former existence of Gondwanaland, the great landmass that is believed to have broken apart to form Africa, Australia, Madagascar, India, South America and the Antarctic continent, and it is certainly true that all the other giant flightless birds – rheas, emus, cassowaries, moas and elephant-birds – once inhabited these areas. Indeed, there appears to be proof of ancestral association between the ostrich and the South American rhea which have identical bird-lice. At first glance the link is not obvious, but bird-lice are very highly specialised, so much so that it is unlikely that they would develop separately and parallel in two distant parts of the world.

The far smaller ancestor of this great bird could almost certainly fly in primeval times. As evidence of this, the ostrich still possesses certain reflexes essential to flight which could never have developed in an entirely earthbound creature. But its terrestrial way of life and vastly increased mass have so modified the ostrich that its atrophied wings and muscles are no longer sufficiently powerful to support it in flight and it must evade its predators, not by burying its head in the sand as tradition would have it, but by running, which it does at speeds of over 50 kilometres an hour.

Besides reducing wing-power, the sheer bulk of the ostrich – the adult male stands 2,5 metres tall and may weigh 160 kilograms – has made various physical adaptations necessary. Whereas most birds defecate and procreate using one bodily opening, the cloaca, the ostrich has developed more sophisticated organs. In smaller birds a simple kidney is sufficient to deal with the liquid intake, but in the ostrich a more specialised excretory system has evolved. And, even without a bladder, this bird is unusual in that it passes urine and faeces separately – though both through the cloaca.

The ostrich is monogamous by circumstance but polygamous should the opportunity arise and a single male sometimes has several females in attendance, one of which is the 'chief wife'. When she has laid her eggs in the nest – a mere scrape in the

91

dry ground – the other wives dutifully follow suit and the clutch may eventually number 20 or more.

By day the females, dull brown in colour to blend with the sandy background, sit on the nest; by night the black and white males take over. The ostrich today is largely confined to the more arid areas where adequate water is at the best of times difficult to find. The female's water and food intake is particularly vital during the breeding and nesting season for she expends extra energy in laying and incubating the eggs. The male relieves her at the nest two or three hours before sunset and she returns to her duties a few hours after dawn when the sap is rising in the succulent grasses she finds to eat. Unless there is a suitable water-hole near by, her entire liquid intake is drawn from these plant juices and the dew that settles on the stems and grass-heads when the cold desert night gives way to the warmth of day. Furthermore, ostriches are sight-feeders and these daylight hours are precious if she is to find food and liquid to sustain her for the rest of the day.

After 40 days of incubation the buff-coloured, bristly-backed chicks emerge. In desert regions the breeding impulse is triggered by the rains and should these persist for months, as occasionally happens, the whole structure of the ostrich community is disrupted. The prolonged sexual drive of the adults creates a situation where the adolescent birds form large leaderless flocks far earlier than would normally be the case and the males among them, perhaps in imitation of the untimely adult behaviour, sometimes appear to resort to homosexual practices. Under normal weather conditions, young ostriches still form flocks, or crèches as they are called, and these are accompanied, guarded and guided by two or three adult birds which, if provoked, can become terrifying creatures. The ferocious power of an ostrich's long legs and the sharp claws of its two-toed foot can inflict savage injuries, to the extent of disembowelling a man. Oddly enough, if the victim defends himself by aggressively waving a stick at the bird's head, this apparently inadequate weapon is often enough to deter the bird for it instinctively protects its prominent eyes on which it is totally dependent to find food. Farmers, knowing that the ostrich fears for its eyes, make for cover in the nearest thorn bush. Another way of avoiding disaster, if all else fails, is to fall flat on the ground where an ostrich cannot kick a man and may merely kneel on his body, allowing him to escape with nothing more serious than a broken rib or two.

91 Eyes that bulge on either side of the ostrich's relatively small head are its most vulnerable spot, for it depends on vision to find food and water. This factor can save a man from vicious attack if he takes cover in a thorn bush or even brandishes a stick aggressively near the bird's eyes. Strategy notwithstanding the ostrich makes a terrifying foe if provoked.

92 The strong resemblance between these ostrich chicks and the dry brown grass common in their arid habitat is a most effective camouflage.

93 Male ostriches on the run. The two-toed foot is an adaptation that enables the bird to make a speedy retreat to escape from danger, the principle being that minimum ground-contact increases speed.

At the beginning of this century ostrich feathers enjoyed immense popularity as adornment for hats and other garments and enormous flocks were kept for their valuable plumage. But fashion is fickle and the advent of the motor car changed things: hats with streaming feathers proved a hazard and ostrich farmers had to resign themselves to less luxurious living. All the same, a steady if considerably smaller demand for ostrich products has continued and although the feathers have never regained their former popularity, there is a ready and consistent market for leather articles made from the attractive and unusual skin – and for biltong from the salted and sun-dried flesh. The eggs, which are still treasured by the Kalahari Bushmen for storing water, are sought-after both as food – each is equivalent to about 24 domestic hen's eggs – and as curios, and ostrich farms in the Oudtshoorn district are extremely popular with tourists who come to gawk at these extraordinary birds.

Yellow-billed Kite

For a raptor, the Yellow-billed Kite has relatively weak talons, and these limit its diet to small animals and food easily obtained. It has even been known to swoop down and flagrantly seize tasty morsels from the open baskets carried by Africans on their heads.

The nests of these birds are among nature's most astonishing nurseries, not structurally, but because of the contents. One is forced to conclude that there is certainly nothing squeamish about the Yellow-billed Kite! A nest once shown me in the southern part of Rhodesia by Valerie Gargett contained plastic bags, chicken feathers, cow-dung, an old belt, dog turds, used lavatory paper, two sanitary towels and a paint-tin lid!

Vultures

The African veld is the natural home of a multitude of mammals – far greater in number than those of the woodland or forest and far more easily visible, dead or alive; therefore, naturally, scavengers and predators are more numerous here, too.

While specialist scavengers like vultures rarely attack living animals a lesser known fact is that predators, from lion to mongoose and from Martial Eagle to Chanting Goshawk, will quite readily eat carrion if they find it.

The vulture is almost universally despised. Its disreputable appearance and habits – although playing a very necessary role in nature's economy – are repulsive. In their favour, however, they are meticulous about washing after feeding. They bathe daily, immersing themselves completely in pools with gently sloping banks where they can come out to dry in the warm sun. During the droughts that so often afflict South Africa this habit can prove fatal: the vultures, deprived of their traditional bathing places, turn to what appears a logical alternative – farm reservoirs. Here they bathe, but afterwards, waterlogged

and unable to take off, they find themselves trapped by the sheer-sided containers and eventually drown.

The White-backed Vulture is a tropical species, replaced farther south by the Cape Vulture. The ranges of the two overlap, and if the bird's white back is not visible it is extremely difficult to distinguish one from the other at a distance. The Cape Vulture is slightly larger and this may in part be explained by the fact that it is a cliff-nester. By using the cliff-face as a launching place its wings are spared some of the effort of lifting such a heavy mass and its greater size is not a disadvantage. On the other hand, loose colonies of White-backed Vultures breed in adjoining trees with sometimes even two nests to a tree.

In the tropics the White-backed is the most numerous species at a carcase but it is generally not the first to approach. Normally it either cruises slowly overhead or alights on a nearby tree to make sure that all is safe. First to move in is the Hooded Vulture which is also the smallest. Once the watching scavengers see that the Hooded Vultures are unmolested, the Lappet-faced, largest and most formidably beaked of all the vulture species, descend and take over, driving other competition away.

Somewhat later, as a rule, the White-backed Vultures arrive on the scene and claim their share. But even the Lappet-faced must give way if the surly Marabou, with its vicious beak, decides to feed. In this way a whole chain of scavengers feeds on the carcase, each in a particular way on some particular part. For instance, the Lappet-faced which arrives early is best-equipped to tear open the body. The White-backed is also expert at opening the carcase and is more likely than the others to get inside to drag out the entrails that it relishes. Subsequent vultures and scavengers get their share until the Hooded Vultures pick the bones and other small birds come to find maggots and blow-flies. Nothing goes waste!

The Cape Vulture is confined to southern Africa and therefore comes into contact with other species only in the extreme north of its range. Its place in the pecking-order at the carcase is dominant where the White-backed is concerned but it, too, gives way to the Lappet-faced and Marabou, if challenged.

Since the beginning of this century the Cape Vulture's numbers have drastically declined. This cannot be blamed totally on man – although farmers dislike these birds for attacking sick or snow-bound sheep and will often shoot them on sight. The steadily decreasing Cape Vulture population is linked to various other factors. Researchers have discovered that the vulture is threatened indirectly by the ever-shrinking herds of game – but not as a diminishing food source. Large predators such as the lion and hyena are becoming scarcer over vast areas of South Africa – indeed they are now largely confined to game reserves and the totally undeveloped areas further north. How does this affect the vulture when livestock and animals still die

94 On the wing a Yellow-bill Kite puts on a dextrous performance, making great use of its long, forked tail to glide, twist and then drop quickly to the ground to snatch at prey.

of natural causes and diseases so that food as such is not in short supply? It has been found that the absence of larger predators to break and grind the bones of the carcase has deprived the vulture chicks of a very important source of calcium. Apparently, adult vultures used to bring bone chips to their nests where the young ate the bits along with the rest of their food. Today, short of calcium, the chicks are rickety and when, at a few months of age, they begin flexing their wings in preparation for flight, their brittle bones break and the birds die. An additional hazard to the Cape Vulture is the overhead high-tension wires with which it may collide. Electrocution, malnutrition, drowning and so on, are creating situations which prevent the Cape Vulture's chicks from reaching adulthood, breeding, and thus ensuring the species.

The Hooded Vulture's share of the carcase is limited to a brief picking at the start and scavenging scraps left on the bones once the more aggressive and larger species have eaten their fill. That it gets in early at all is a result of its small size. Vultures, like many other large birds, depend on thermals to gain altitude and thus rise late in the morning. The Hooded requires less lift than its bulkier competitors and it is up earliest, giving it a chance to feed on carcases before other vultures are up and about. Of course, once the sun is fully risen, the Lappet-faced and White-backed take over and the Hooded must wait patiently for the scraps. Perhaps for this reason it is less dependent on carrion as a source of food than the other vulture species. The Hooded will catch lizards, winged termites and small creatures to supplement its diet. It also scavenges round

villages and fishing camps and, in West Africa, even dares to enter the towns; but the South African urban sanitary system is too efficient for it to make much of living in built-up areas.

95 A dour Lappet-faced Vulture incubates her clutch. Her naked head, a feature common to most species of vulture, is bare to lessen the chances of contamination by putrefying flesh – despite the fact that all these birds bathe daily!

96 The perfect example of the opportunist predator! A resentful Hooded Vulture, first at the kill early in the morning, is driven off by this young lion.

97 If the vulture has any trait worthy of respect it is its supreme mastery of the art of flying. Soaring high on thermals, it scans the countryside below for signs of carrion. The Cape Vulture is one of a species that is being endangered chiefly by malnutrition, electrocution and drowning.

98 White-backed Vultures crowd and jostle at a kill. It is fascinating to see the rapid arrival of dozens of these scavengers at a kill after the first vulture has made the discovery. The message travels very quickly for in the air the vulture's strongly marked black and white plumage makes it readily visible to its fellows. No sooner does one bird spot carrion and begin its descent than the others, as if at a signal, dip their wings and converge for their share. It is an efficient method, the birds searching collectively over a far wider area than would be possible alone.

99 Vultures wait patiently on an acacia thorn tree for thermals on which they will wing away in their ceaseless search for food.

99

Sandgrouse

Many birds do not have to drink at all – they draw all their liquid requirements from the food they eat. The Sandgrouse however prefers to live in arid areas where it feeds on dry seeds which contain very little moisture and it must therefore drink daily. Vast flocks assemble at water-holes at dusk and dawn, each species arriving at a specific time. The choice of hour is obvious for the Sandgrouse may have to fly 50 kilometres or more to its watering-place and at morning and evening the air is coolest. Predators, bird and beast, are fully aware of the Sandgrouse's synchronous drinking habits and sit in wait near by. But the birds, flocking in their hundreds, 'hide in a crowd', using their sheer weight of numbers to inhibit attack and relying on a thousand eyes to warn of danger more effectively than any single bird could.

The Namaqua Sandgrouse must drink daily and its distribution in desert areas depends totally on the presence of water. Therefore it is nomadic and has evolved a method of carrying water over long distances to its young. In a particular structural and behavioural adaptation the adult saturates its specially modified breast-feathers at the pool and then flies back to the young who nibble at its breast, releasing and drinking the water at the same time.

100 Hundreds of Double-banded Sandgrouse drink at a water-hole at dusk. Predators wait for this regular daily occurrence that may provide an easy meal: however, the jostling crowds of birds are not such a simple target and their sheer numbers prove a form of defence.

101 Flocking to their morning drink, these Namaqua Sandgrouse will carry water in their soaked breast-feathers to chicks waiting in the desert dunes.

100

101

Eagles

The Eagle is popularly recognised as the king of birds of prey and in keeping with this image it actively hunts for most of its food. But lesser-known is the fact that it will sometimes join vultures at a carcase.

One of southern Africa's finest eagles is the Black or Verreaux's. A pair of these handsome birds will preside over a vast territory in mountainous countryside. Here, along the cliff-edges, they build as many as four nests and breed in one or another in different years. Sometimes they prefer to use the same nest for several years in succession, but the nest is always refurbished before breeding begins. By adding new material annually – including sprays of fresh leaves – the nest eventually becomes a very big structure indeed.

The Black Eagle is essentially a food specialist: over 90% of its diet is made up of dassies (rock-rabbits) which compete in many areas with sheep for grazing. Unfortunately, farmers tend to overlook this, and instead of regarding the eagle as a friend remember the odd lamb it may have taken. Nowadays, however, a more enlightened view prevails and the eagle is protected by law.

Nowhere is the Black Eagle more prevalent than in the Matopos Hills near Bulawayo, Rhodesia. Here each pair rules an area of up to 1 000 hectares or more, and feeds on the dassies that inhabit the granite kopjes.

Black Eagle nestlings engage in a 'Cain and Abel' conflict that always ends with one chick dead (the normal clutch consists of two). The first hatched has time to gather strength before it is joined by its sibling, and then persistently savages the younger bird until it is killed.

Originally this was explained in terms of a shortage of food, but a bitter conflict and death of one chick has been observed at a nest which was littered with food. The outcome of the battle is obviously an automatic part of the eagle's breeding pattern. It is therefore all the more strange that the eagle lays two eggs if only one is to survive. The most likely explanation is that the second egg is purely an insurance policy against anything happening to the first, and once one chick has made its appearance the other egg and its contents are superfluous.

The Tawny Eagle is a wide-ranging species found throughout Africa – except in heavy forest – in southern Europe and as far east as India. In the extreme south of the African continent it has been largely shot and destroyed, though it is still occasionally spotted in the Karoo.

Small birds and mammals, including hares, francolins and guinea-fowl, are this bird's prey. But these are not its sole source of food; it will rob other predators of their victims and take carrion when available.

Like most other larger birds of prey, the Tawny Eagle is a winter breeder. Thus, when the time comes for it to feed its young the annual grass-fires that ravage vast areas of the African veld have run their course, and without groundcover hunting is that much easier. Timing is all the more important in view of the eagle's comparatively long incubation – over a month. Smaller birds of prey, with shorter incubation periods, can afford to nest later: to breed earlier would for them be unproductive since the young would hatch when the groundcover was still dense and food consequently more difficult to locate.

An active and rapacious predator of smaller animals and birds, domestic poultry included, is the African Hawk Eagle. Its range extends even further than the Tawny's for it is found in southern Europe (where it is known as Bonelli's Eagle) and eastward to southern China. This bird most often hunts with its mate near by and puts on a performance remarkable for verve and style considering its relatively small size. Its most frequent technique is to dash from cover to snatch up its unsuspecting victim, but like all other raptors, it will also stoop on its prey from the air. All the same it is not one to overlook a ready meal: one day a fire swept close to a nest I was photographing and within hours the charred remains of two cane-rats and a korhaan were brought to the chick.

The nest is used year after year, becoming ever larger in the process. Incubation is the female's work and the male brings her food to the nest, although she will hunt for her own if he temporarily relieves her from her duties. The young often fight bitterly but the result is not as invariably fatal to the nestlings as in the case of the Black Eagle. Nest-viewing of this species is only for the intrepid; the nest is high in a tree and the parents boldly defend their young and have been known to attack people climbing up for closer inspection. Seldom do male and female eagles stay long together at the nest when in use for rearing young. It seems that the presence of food in the nest excites competition between mates and, since the female is larger than the male, confrontation is avoided by few meetings in this situation.

The Bateleur has been described as 'the most magnificent and characteristic bird of the skies'. And anyone who has seen it on the wing, gliding fast across the sky, frequently rocking from side to side mid-flight, will instantly recognise it. Nothing could be more exciting than this bird streaking overhead, with its very short tail and curved wings etched in the sky like a Cupid's bow.

Bateleurs belong to one or other of two 'morphs', those with

102 Scanning the veld below, its wing-tip feathers splayed by the downward sweep of the wings, a Black Eagle soars aloft to hunt.

103 An adult Black Eagle tends its victorious offspring. Sole occupant of a nest that originally held two eggs, this chick has fought and won a death-struggle with its sibling rival. Exposed in its open nest to the full heat of the sun, this four-day old chick shelters in the shade cast by its parent's body.

chestnut backs and those with cream backs and the incidence of these varies geographically. In Zambia the chestnut-backed predominate in the ratio of ten to one, but in South Africa the cream-backs are virtually unknown, although the reason for this polymorphism is an absolute mystery.

What the Bateleur eats has been the subject of controversy. It cannot be disputed that it will eat carrion, but it is equally certain that it also takes live prey. I have myself heard agonising squeals from a dog after a Bateleur has stooped in the vicinity and there are endless records of its taking cane-rats, young jackals, snakes, birds and even the large *Cetina* snails. More amazingly, I once found the skull of a lion cub in a Bateleur's nest!

These birds lay only one egg, need huge territories, breed in summer and place their nests below the canopy of the trees in which they nest. In all these points they differ from the great majority of other eagles. The chick, when hatched, is brown and remains that colour until it is almost mature at six to eight years of age. This is yet another feature that sets the Bateleur apart from most other eagles whose chicks are white when hatched. Exactly what inferences to draw are not known, but it is essential that this bird be studied soon for it is today found in South Africa only in protected national parks.

Knowing that Bateleur Eagles desert their nests at even the most cautious human approach, I had to make elaborate arrangements before the unique photograph of a sitting female could

104

be taken. First we built a wooden model of a camera which we bolted to the next tree, about 10 metres away from the nest. Once the bird was accustomed to the dummy we replaced it with the real thing which was camouflaged, sound-proofed and equipped with radio so that exposures could be made from up to 2 kilometres away. Even this arrangement had its hazards, for mud-wasps made a hole through the camouflage bag and fouled up the release mechanism. In the final analysis the experiment was only a partial success for no sooner was the chick hatched than a pair of Ground Hornbills appeared on the scene and made short work of it. Needless to say the adult Bateleur soon flew off and our efforts were not fully rewarded.

104 Wings spread to shade her chick, an African Hawk Eagle glares over her shoulder at her approaching mate. An audacious hunter, the Hawk Eagle will either dash among the trees, flushing out its prey before finally killing it on the ground, or perch motionless for hours waiting for a likely victim.

105 Its sharp beak outlined by the dying sun, this Hawk Eagle stands beside its chick. The golf-ball sized crop, visible below the youngster's beak, is evidence that it has recently enjoyed a good meal.

106 The Tawny Eagle's riveting stare seems to epitomize the expression 'eagle-eyed'. Poised high overhead, the bird's superb eyesight picks out victims on the ground – or carrion, if it is available.

107 Its beak scimitar-shaped for cutting flesh, a young African Hawk Eagle gazes steadfastly into the distance.

108 The Bateleur's coral red beak and legs identify it when perching as surely as its crescent wings do when in flight.

109 Knowing that Bateleur Eagles desert their nests at even the most cautious human approach, I had to make elaborate arrangements before this unique photograph could be taken. However, the experiment was not entirely successful, for a pair of Ground Hornbills made short work of the newborn chick and the mother then deserted the nest.

110 A rock-splitter fig tree, growing from a fissure between granite boulders provides this Augur Buzzard with a nesting-site in the Motopos Hills, Rhodesia.

111 As one, this pair of Jackal Buzzards peer from their cliff-edge nest. Flying high, they will grapple, lock and tumble together mid-air in a breath-taking act that reinforces the pair bond.

Buzzards

Characteristic of South Africa's bird fauna is the number of species dependent on rocks, cliffs and mountains. Among many other birds of prey whose way of life is bound up with hills, are Jackal and Augur Buzzards which, although closely related, are not found simultaneously in any one area. In America the term 'buzzard' is applied to what are known as vultures in South Africa, and the bird I refer to here as a buzzard is somewhat smaller than an eagle which it resembles in the way it lives. Broad-winged masters of soaring flight, they capture their prey by stooping from the air or by pouncing from a perch. For their food they depend largely on the numerous small mammals, reptiles and birds that inhabit the veld, but at the same time they are not above feeding off animals killed by speeding vehicles on nearby roads.

The Jackal Buzzard and his mate maintain their own territory and will chase off, in no uncertain manner, any bird that encroaches on their domain – irrespective of the intruder's size. In aerial display to reinforce the pair bond, the male soars above the female, gradually descending towards her, calling all the while. Then, both birds hold their wings above their backs, hang down their feet and, as the male approaches, the female will often roll on her back and grapple her claws to his.

Swallows

Still largely true to its ancestral haunts in krantz and kloof, is the Cliff Swallow, although like other southern African species it has adapted to nesting against walls, under bridges, and so on. This is a colonial bird, a flock building anything from a dozen to several hundred semi-globular mud-nests, their outward-facing entrances at the top and their sides often overlapping. The number of birds tends to vary from year to year and there may be some interchange between the colonies when the flocks arrive from the north for breeding in August. There are two broods each season and, on average, three young are reared by each pair of adults. Should the nests be broken down during the winter when the birds are absent from southern Africa, the time wasted on rebuilding may well limit the adults to a single brood, especially if the rains are late and mud not immediately available.

Successful Cliff Swallows tend to congregate in the middle of the colony where they will be protected by other nests, and thus several seasons' experience is a decided advantage. They compete for the safest nests and the birds breeding in these positions are notably those that return to the colony first after migration in order to have the pick of the best spots.

Swallows, swifts and martins are all aerial feeders. This sort of activity burns up a great deal of energy which these birds replace by feeding constantly. Their short beaks and wide mouths enable them, while on the wing, to snap up large numbers of passing insects which provide a rich source of energy vital for birds that constantly speed about.

Mountain Chat

The adult Mountain Chat displays a most remarkable polymorphism. The females, dark grey with white rumps and outer tail-feathers, are all alike, but the males vary considerably from grey to black, though they always have white tail-feathers.

This chat is strongly territorial: it claims possession with song and then advertises ownership by ostentatiously posing on rocks. It often appears near houses where it becomes quite tame, and on a farm in the Maltahöhe district of South West Africa two pairs parcelled out the yard between them and not only chased each other if they trespassed but also drove off Karoo and Familiar Chats that dared intrude.

Rocks also provide a good vantage point from which to watch for insects either passing in the air or moving about in the ground-litter. In addition, the varying plumages of these birds blend with light and shade in rocky areas fissured with dark crevices.

Lilac-breasted Roller

Tree-hole nesting is common among South African birds but few beside the woodpecker can make their own. This means that the availability of suitable holes limits the numbers of birds that are obliged to use them and competition, both among birds of the same species and between those of different species but having the same tree-hole nesting habits, is intense.

Abundant and most widespread of the larger birds that use tree-holes is the Lilac-breasted Roller, also known as Mzilikazi's Roller because the famous Ndebele chief claimed it his sole right to wear its gaudy feathers. In the open veld and light woodland where it lives, it is a bold and noisy bird that does not hesitate to attack hawks and eagles which intrude on its territory.

In the air its antics during courtship-display flights endorse its name, roller – though unlike the European species, it does not make a complete roll, the performance being more like a series of wobbly dives.

Purple Roller

The Purple Roller is rather more heavily-built than the Lilac-breasted and, while it shares the same geographical range, it is a rarer bird. It is a summer breeding migrant to South Africa vanishing, no one knows where, in about April. With the third species of roller, the Racket-tailed, these birds inhabit the country according to the density of trees: the *Brachystegia* woodland or *miombo* is the Racket-tailed's domain; the open acacia woodland, where there are slightly more trees than suit the Lilac-breasted, is the Purple's habitat.

Perhaps the Purple Roller's diet covers the broadest spectrum of the three species: it includes tough and distasteful items such as scorpions, hard-cased beetles, millipedes and the brightly-coloured locusts which most birds will not touch. It is also extremely garrulous, and noisily chases off almost every bird that dares intrude into its immediate feeding area. Rollers all sit on trees and bushes, closely watching the ground until something edible comes into view; then down they flash with bright wings to snatch it up. It is possible that the Purple Roller's brilliant colours hide it from insects, as does the Bee-eater's aggressive camouflage make it an effective hunter.

The rollers nest in tree-holes but, unlike hornbills which almost completely seal the entrances, they leave theirs open thus exposing themselves and their clutch to attack from predators. However, parent and brood are far less vulnerable lodged in the trunk of a tree than species that nest in the open.

112 Their own nest complete, a pair of Cliff Swallows watch other birds in the colony compete for suitable breeding-sites. This complicated structure consists of some 1 500 mud pellets, each mixed with saliva, carried one by one and cemented together to create the Cliff Swallow's home.

113 Tail streamers showing the course of its flight, a Lesser Striped Swallow flashes by in a neat turn.

114 An insect in the mouth is not enough; this male Mountain Chat hops on to a rock to make sure he does not miss any other passing prey.

115 The little Wire-tailed Swallow breeds near water where there is mud suitable for building its half-bowl nests. The pipe of a river pump makes an ideal spot from which to hawk insects carried by air currents across the water.

Crowned Plover

Only the larger plovers inhabit dry land, for the smaller species are basically waterside birds. Most widespread of the open country plovers is the Crowned, a pugnacious and vigorous bird which is shown in the photograph pluckily defending its ground nest from the huge trampling feet of a White Rhinoceros. More commonly, the Crowned Plover will, during the nesting season, mob intruders from the air, diving and circling over and over again while uttering the high-pitched screams from which its Afrikaans name 'Kiewietjie' comes. Any sort of really open country suits this plover and it is one of the few species that will venture into the forbidding wastes of the Namib Desert.

Carmine Bee-eater

Few will refute that the Carmine Bee-eater is the most beautiful bird in Africa. It is a migrant to the south where it breeds each year, its spectacular colonies transforming the nesting site into a roiling blaze of colour. This bird nests in holes which it drives into the vertical banks of rivers, but the sheer volume of numbers often means that some of the birds must overflow on to the flat land above so that here the tunnels are driven in at a downward-sloping angle.

Some of the colonies are famous among bird-lovers all over the world and one particular breeding site on the banks of the Chobe River in Botswana is a major tourist drawcard. Indeed, any one of its larger nesting places along the Zambezi, Chobe and Okavango Rivers is worth visiting, the whole bank a blaze of crimson during the season. Besides the visual splendour of breeding Carmine Bee-eaters, they are additionally unusual in that members of the family unit rally to care for the young – the 'children of previous marriages' all pitching in to help.

After the breeding season they move north into the tropics of East Africa where they roam about, still in flocks, often feasting off the insects driven from bush fires. During the dry non-breeding season the Carmine Bee-eaters pursue an activity not unlike that of the Cattle Egret. They often ride on the backs of grazing animals which flush out insects hidden in the grass and the birds then swoop down and catch them. Incredibly, they even use the great Kori Bustard, itself a bird, for this purpose.

There is a theory, yet to be proven, that this bird uses a form of aggressive camouflage. Its plumage, brilliantly coloured to human eyes, may well be less visible to the bees and insects on which it feeds and in this way the bird is a more effective hunter.

116 Perfectly placed on an airy perch, a Lilac-breasted Roller watches for passing insect trade.

117

118

117 Skilfully holding a large scorpion by its head and pincers, a Purple Roller bashes the creature's dangerous jabbing tail on an acacia branch. This bird makes a meal of many insects rejected by other birds as being either too big, too dangerous or too distasteful.

118 Undeterred by the difference in size, a Crowned Plover gamely takes on a grazing rhinoceros that threatens to trample the bird's ground-level nest near by. By throwing its wings in the air to seem larger, rending the air with strident calls and rushing at its enormous adversary, the bird succeeded in diverting the lumbering beast.

119 Cocking backwards and forwards, a Black Korhaan steps daintily across the veld. Its striking plumage is intended to advertise that the bird is unappetising, for black and white in combination warn off predators with a message: 'I'm not tasty, leave me alone!'. Animals like the skunk, porcupine and Honey Badger, among others, display these warning colours.

120 This sequence of photographs endorses a fact that few will dispute: that the Carmine Bee-eater is the most beautiful of southern Africa's birds. Brilliantly coloured to human eyes, bee-eaters may well be less visible to the bees and other insects on which they feed. There is a theory, yet to be finally proven, that these birds use a form of aggressive camouflage. What appears, say, scarlet to us may register completely differently on the bee retina. Indeed, the Carmine Bee-eater's flagrant colouring may possibly camouflage it from its victim and make the bird a more effective hunter.

121 The river bank pocked with burrows, a Carmine Bee-eater pauses before entering its nesting hole.

138

123

124

122 In brilliant crimson and black nuptial attire, the Red Bishop puffs out his feathers in a courtship display. It is only in the breeding season that the male assumes his spectacular colouring and risks being conspicuous; for the rest of the year his plumage resembles that of the demure brown speckled female.

123 Wings spread, a White-throated Swallow pauses momentarily to push food down the beak of a beckoning chick.

124 The brilliant yellow gape of the Banded Sand Martin chick provides an obvious target for the parent bringing food to the nest. At the same time, the bright gape visually stimulates the adult to collect food and thrust it into the waiting mouth. A closed beak means a satisfied stomach and the adult automatically ceases its feeding efforts.

Trees and Woodland

There is considerable geological evidence that part of southern Africa was once covered by large tracts of forest – even the now arid Kalahari appears to have sheltered under the protection of leafy vegetation in ages past. However, for its size, southern Africa today is singularly poor in true forest – but it is not without trees. The tall umbrella-shaped *Brachystegia*, the stunted acacia, stout baobabs and a host of other species give shade and sustenance to bird and beast. Birds roost in the trees and some, like the weavers, adorn the branches with gigantic tenement-block nests. Others feed on the fruits and nest in hollows and holes in the trunk. And wherever trees thrive, so do the birds.

Cape Turtle Dove

From Cape Agulhas to Uganda the Cape Turtle Dove's rolling call 'How's Father? How's Father?' is heard everywhere within flying distance of water and outside of evergreen forests. It is, in fact, among the most numerous and widespread of all southern African birds.

Because large numbers of individual birds will gather at water-holes or some abundant feeding place, it is mistakenly believed to be generally gregarious. On the contrary, these assemblies are not flocks in the true sense. Normally the Cape Turtle Dove lives in pairs, the birds keeping very much to themselves except when drawn together by some particularly rich feeding area or to a common drinking site. Admittedly, if danger approaches the doves may rise as one with a roar of wings, but they otherwise function individually. Their constant comings and goings at the beginning and end of the day at a drinking place clearly illustrate the error in the thinking that each bird is anything but a completely independent entity.

Cape Turtle Doves feed almost exclusively on seeds taken on the ground; yet to roost and nest they must have trees. The result is that they commute between the woodlands where they breed and roost and the open country where they forage. In addition, the very limited water-content of their staple fare also means they must remain within flying distance of a drinking-place at all times.

Man's alterations to the environment have often suited the dove well. Large-scale cultivation provides plenty of weed seeds and the opportunity to glean in the grain fields, too; and in what were relatively tree-less areas before, man has planted forests in which the dove can now roost and nest.

All doves feed their young on a secretion called pigeon's milk that oozes from the lining of the crop. To find this rich food-source, the ravenous young must reach into the parent's mouth. People undertaking the tedious task of rearing orphan doves must substitute the natural food with a mixture of baby cereal and milk, and then feed the chick with this, a drop at a time, throughout the day.

Parrots

Compared to South America and Australia, Africa has few species of parrot. With the exception of Meyer's Parrot, which is fairly prevalent in woodland areas, there are only two species of lovebird within southern African limits and four larger parrots in all.

Meyer's Parrot is entirely vegetarian, seeds and wild fruits – especially figs – are the mainstay of its diet. Only sometimes will it leave the safety of the woodlands to feed on grain, but in such small numbers that it hardly constitutes a threat to crops. Indeed, the only 'problem parrot' in the southern African farming context is the Rosy-faced Lovebird.

Small parties of Meyer's Parrot fly swiftly through the woodlands, their raucous screeching and high-pitched clinking keeping them in touch in a habitat where visibility is severely hampered by dense foliage and the dappled shade of trees. On the wing, the bird avoids trees and branches with magnificent agility, and when it alights to feed it is a masterful acrobat, using beak and feet to move easily on and around branches. The parrot's strong beak proves a versatile tool, perfectly adapted to stripping fruits, cracking nuts and even acting as a third leg or foot if needed when the bird manoeuvres in its tree-top habitat. In the heights of the forest canopy, agility, speed and superb camouflage keep the Meyer's Parrot a step ahead of predators.

The breeding adult lays two eggs and, using its tough beak, keeps the aperture of the nesting-hole open when the growing tree extends its cambium layer and threatens to constrict the opening.

125 The Little Bee-eater stretches a wing in delicate contrast to an angular tracery of wire. As its name implies, it is the smallest species of this group of birds in southern Africa. During the breeding season seldom seen far from its nest which it digs in a bank, it perches near the ground so that the insects on which it feeds are silhouetted against the sky.

126 Pausing as it drinks, a Cape Turtle Dove checks for predators. It is one of very few species that need not lift its head to swallow with each sip of water. Birds that sip keep a watch-out with each lift of their heads, but pigeons, doves, and one or two other species that can suck up water and swallow continuously, drink quickly so that they need not waste time at the drinking-place where all birds are particularly vulnerable.

127 Perched on a 'nibbling' post where it sharpens and cleans its beak, this Meyer's Parrot flashes yellow 'elbow' feathers.

128 Despite its delightful name, the Laughing Dove, this bird may prove a serious indication of the dire conditions in which we live. Bones of specimens from urban areas have been found to contain up to ten times more lead than those that live in the country. Although the source of this dangerous substance has not been definitely linked to motor-car exhaust fumes this bird may prove a harbinger of the dangers that man's continued abuse of the environment may bring.

128

129 Massed at the water's edge, Cape Turtle Doves arrive for a drink. Drawn only by common habits and the hide-In-a-crowd instinct, they are not in fact true flocking birds, each one coming and going independently.

130 The art of camouflage is brought to fine pitch by this Scops Owl concealed by its cryptic colouring against a perfectly matching tree.

130

Owls

The owl is a bird of the night. Hoping to be left in peace during the day, it depends on its cryptically patterned and coloured plumage for effective camouflage against the tree trunks where it roosts. If, however, it is spotted by the small birds which it frequently victimises, they play tit-for-tat by mobbing the sleeping predator and disturbing its rest.

The owl's head is superbly adjusted to its nocturnal ways. The large staring eyes can perceive shapes in even the dimmest light, although the owl does not depend mainly on vision to hunt. Lighter-shaded circular areas surrounding the actual eye act as giant reflectors and indeed the entire face can be likened to a radar disc swivelling through 200° on the bird's amazingly supple neck. Set side by side on the flat face, the eyes also provide depth-perception vital as the bird flies down to snatch prey already pin-pointed by sound.

Hearing is the owl's chief hunting device. Its ears are placed asymmetrically on either side of the head in disc-like depressions for funnelling sound. Silently swivelling its head around in the dark, the owl can catch the slightest scuffling of an animal or bird and by triangulation locates its prey exactly. Then, using its eyes as an additional guide, it swoops down in the dark to claim its meal.

A big bird, the Giant Eagle-owl includes in its diet hefty items like hare and guinea-fowl, and the pellets of indigestible food that it regurgitates after feeding give a good idea of its regular fare – wing-cases of beetles, feathers, large bones and so on are all common. The Giant Eagle-owl's pale colouring accounts for its other name, 'Milky Owl' – repeated in its Latin specific name *lacteus* meaning milk – but the reason for this light colour is as yet unknown.

On account of its nocturnal habits, the small Scops Owl is rarely seen. I managed to lure the specimen in the photograph close enough to my camera only by playing a recording of its trilling cricket-like chirp. Illuminated by the silvery sheen from my flash, one curious feature stands out – the pair of feather tufts on its head which look like ears but in fact have nothing to do with hearing. The Giant Eagle-owl, too, displays this strange headgear which is an excellent example of visual mimicry. Presumably, birds contemplating disturbing the owl during the day confuse the shape of its head with that of one of the cat family and are warned off.

The Scops has an immense range which includes the whole of Africa (except, today, the south-west), southern Europe and most of Asia, and must therefore be a highly successful bird. It is not surprising in a range this size that the bird displays a good deal of variation in plumage colour. Some of the differentiation can be accounted for geographically, but not all: the two major colour groups, one predominantly brown and the other predominantly grey, occur throughout the bird's range.

131 Seemingly sleepy-eyed here, the Giant Eagle-owl has vision that is superbly adapted to its nocturnal habits. Even on the darkest nights the large binocular eyes can perceive the birds and mammals on which it feeds. Bristles clustered on either side of the beak keep food out of the large vulnerable eyes, and the light-coloured patches concentrate light in the visual areas of the face.

132 Raising a pair of chicks is unusual for the Giant Eagle-owl, although it lays two eggs. The youngsters have prodigious appetites and the parents keep up a non-stop supply of food. In a single night I saw a boomslang, several francolins, a large Rhino Beetle and a nightjar delivered to the nest by the hard-working parents.

133 Illuminated by the silvery sheen of my flash, one feature of the Scops Owl stands out – the tufts of feathers on its head which look like ears but in fact have nothing to do with hearing. This is an excellent example of visual mimicry. During the day when the owl sleeps, birds tempted to disturb it are presumably warned off by the resemblance between the owl's head and that of a cat.

134 Unusual for venturing out during the daylight hours, the small Pearl-spotted Owl peers from its well-protected nesting-hole. Here it will lay its clutch of three which, like all owls' eggs, are pure white.

135 In early spring a Red-headed Weaver builds its nest from supple new shoots of the Bastard Marula. During summer the twigs will dry out and toughen, creating a home almost impregnable to predators.

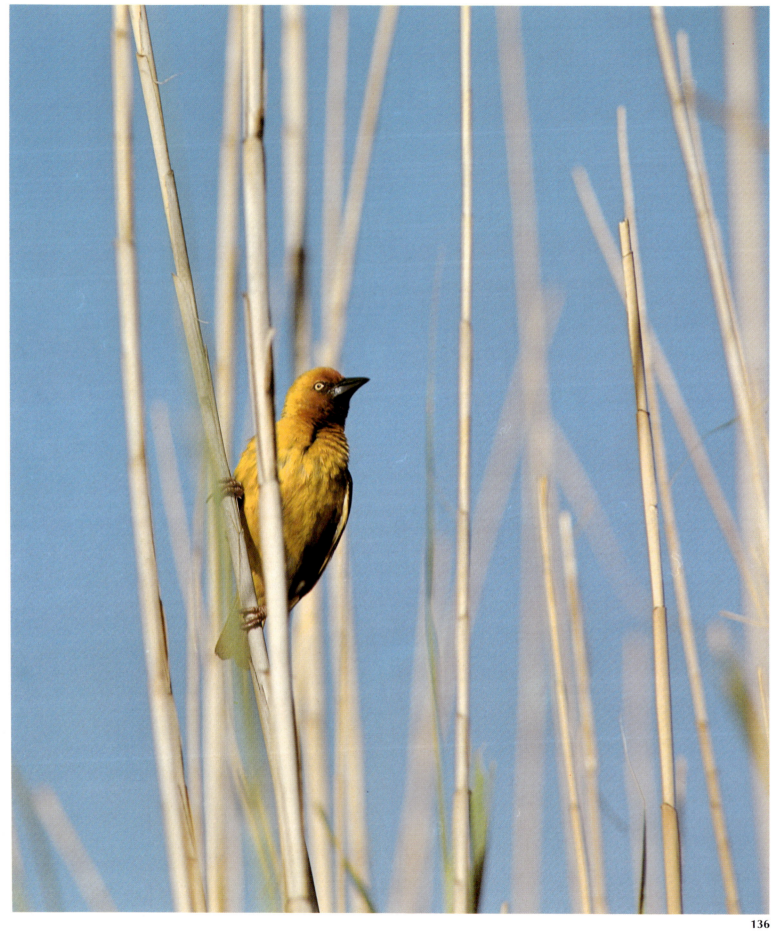

136 Alert to danger, a male Cape Weaver examines a potential nesting site.

137 Pied Crows are often first at a kill – not surprisingly since they are so common and always on the look-out for the main chance! This bird pecks greedily at the remains of a wildebeest killed by marauding wild dogs.

137

Weavers

At the first sign of spring the male Red-headed Weaver gets down to the business of home-building. In the woodlands where this species lives, grass is in short supply. Instead, the male plucks the supple new shoots of the Bastard Marula and skilfully weaves them into a ball-shaped nest with long entrance-tunnel. During the hot summer months that follow, the shoots dry out and toughen until the weaver's nest becomes a veritable stronghold. Although in open view on a branch, and despite its colourful occupants, it provides a predator-proof and durable shelter. Large predators find it simply too hard to handle, and smaller ones are deterred by its densely packed structure. Only occasionally will a bird like the Bush Shrike manage to work its beak through the nest wall and reach the inner sanctum.

The male Red-headed Weaver has several mates – yellow in plumage where he is red – each with her own home which she helps to construct from the inside. Retort-shaped when complete, the long entrance tunnel is probably intended to discourage snakes. However, the Red-headed Weaver is more successful in baffling predators when he builds his nest from telephone wires. Even hawks and owls must find this additionally frustrating.

Once the rains have broken the male Cape Weaver sets about claiming a suitable breeding-site and shortly afterwards begins to build a large kidney-shaped structure as his nest. But before the females accept his offer of a protected territory near an ample food supply, they also inspect the accommodation and only if it meets with their approval will they go on to line it and breed. Once he has won his first mate, the male continues to enlarge his home adding extra nests in the hope of attracting more females. Even if he does not succeed in this his efforts will not be wasted for he and his offspring use the additional nests for roosting.

The weaving instinct in these industrious birds must be strong, as a tale told by some friends illustrates. Birds in their garden often settled on a wire-netting fence *en route* to a feeding table near by. One day a mousebird perched on the wire, its long graceful tail sweeping down decoratively and proving an irresistible attraction to a passing weaver which immediately began weaving the long tail-feathers into the netting – much to the annoyance of the mousebird!

Probably the industrious bird was a young male for weaving is an imprinted skill. There is a crucial period, normally a few months after fledging, when the youngsters must practise and perfect their weaving if they are to become proficient. If for any reason during this vital period the bird is deprived of, say, materials as was done in a series of experiments, it never develops the skill – no matter that it was later given ample material and could observe others at work.

To judge by appearances, the Social Weaver is a common-place little bird but its looks belie it. There is certainly nothing ordinary about its gigantic tenement-block nests which are so substantial that they can remain in continuous use for a century or more. The natural building-site is a tree, usually an acacia or aloe (kokerboom), but telephone poles provide a suitable modern alternative, and because of this the weaver has been able to extend its range.

It begins nest-building by placing strong twigs on a branch or pole and skilfully intertwining them to create a dome. Straw is used to fill in the structure and form the smaller apartments. At the entrance stiff stalks pointing inwards deter predators – or human hands – from intruding. The weaver lays its eggs in a rounded chamber but even after the breeding season the communal nest continues to be the centre of its activities. Every night it returns there to roost though the nesting apartments are no longer the exclusive property of any one pair. Thatching is recognised as an effective insulator and in the desert regions where these birds live their huge straw edifices protect them from intense cold by night and searing heat by day.

Within the tenement there is a definite social organisation: nests are grouped into sub-colonies and birds from one do not trespass on the premises of another. There are, however, a number of uninvited guests. The lovely little Rosy-faced Lovebirds and equally charming Pygmy Falcons not only breed there but make use of the nest for roosting, often to the righteous indignation of the weavers. Another gate-crasher is the Red-headed Finch but, being a winter-breeder, its activities do not clash with those of the weaver which appears to tolerate its presence with a degree of equanimity.

But chief among the Social Weaver's enemies is the dreaded Black-necked Cobra. Performing the most astonishing acrobatic contortions, it slithers from chamber to chamber, making short work of the eggs and young of an entire colony. No doubt the weavers are safer from this threat when their home is hung aloft a telephone pole, but then they have to contend with possible demolition by an unsympathetic Department of Posts and Telegraphs.

Pied Crow

The Pied Crow's catholic taste in food accounts for its success in habitats as varied as the southern Sahara and the equatorial forests of the Congo. It is completely omnivorous and anything remotely edible provides a feast, be it offal or carrion, eggs or nestlings, grain, insects or small mammals. Wherever man lives the Pied Crow congregates. Along main roads it gathers to scavenge birds and animals killed by speeding motorists, and it is always on the look-out for the main chance. Chicks in the poultry yard, fish on drying racks, and kitchen scraps are all sources of food. It is accused, with justice, of pecking out the eyes of sick or injured sheep and it is hardly surprising with all these misdemeanours to its credit that it is generally hated – yet it continues to prosper.

One reason for this is that it combines boldness with wary cunning. It will nonchalantly eat carrion on the road until a car is almost on top if it, but let the car slow down and it is off before the driver can stop. It soon learns to recognise a gun and keeps well away when one is in sight; as for traps, these usually prove inadequate for this quick-witted bird.

The Pied Crow normally nests in trees but will, however, use telephone poles as a substitute, and even windmills – its nesting-material fouling up the mechanism and adding another item against it to the farmer's list. The actual nest is of sticks but the bird often incorporates bits of fencing wire and, in one incredible instance, the entire nest was made of this decidedly uncomfortable material.

Oxpeckers

Oxpeckers are an avian oddity. As their name indicates, they perch on domestic stock and game animals, particularly buffalo and giraffe, so that they can gorge themselves on ticks and blood-sucking flies and even nibble at open sores. They are curious and agile birds, their short legs and sharp claws enabling them to clamber nimbly over the backs and sides of their hosts, often clinging on, woodpecker-like, or propping themselves up with their stiff tail-feathers. Their laterally flattened beaks shear ticks off the animal's hide and probe eagerly into its ears, nostrils and around its eyes in search of food. Often they work together in parties, warning their host of the approach of a hunter by rising from their perch with a loud rattling cry of alarm.

There are only two species – the Yellow-billed and the Red-billed – which are peculiar to Africa though they are rarely, if ever, seen south of the Transvaal and Natal. Once they were abundant wherever there were herds of grazing animals, but the custom of cattle-dipping has led to a decline in their numbers, either because they devoured poisoned ticks, or because the reduction in tick population deprived them of their food-supply. Today they limit their attentions to game and occasionally find a welcome host in cattle. They nest in tree-holes, a whole host of helpers caring for the new brood.

Oxpeckers are host-specific and the two species tend to direct their attention to certain animals rather than others depending on one factor – 'hairiness'. The Red-billed has a definite preference for more hirsute hosts such as various species of antelope, while the Yellow-billed prefers to feed off creatures such as buffalo that are relatively less hairy.

Grey Lourie

Generations of hunters have been infuriated by the Grey Lourie's harsh onomatopoeic cry of alarm from which it gets its popular name 'Go-away Bird'. Game animals understand only too well what is afoot and heed the warning. Not satisfied with this, the Grey Lourie flutters and jumps about in the trees at a safe distance from the intruder, raising and lowering its crest in agitation and protesting loudly until the hunter gives up in despair.

This is a bird of the veld and a member of the remarkable touraco family peculiar to Africa. Among this group's curious features is its green colouring, present only in traces in the Grey Lourie.

This bird rarely descends to the ground, preferring to fly slowly from tree to tree but becoming nimble on foot among the branches. An exclusive vegetarian, it eats fruit which may be highly poisonous to man; for example one of its favourites is the berries of the tree popularly known as syringa. If a child eats these, they sometimes prove fatal but that the lourie does so with impunity needs explanation. The syringa berry in itself may not be poisonous; it is the hard seed that is toxic. Louries, like many other birds, simply digest the fruit and then pass the seed intact and are therefore unharmed.

Cape Sparrow

Bold, jaunty and impudent, the Cape Sparrow, or 'Mossie', is familiar both in town and country. With his demure and devoted mate, at the beginning of winter he builds his disgracefully untidy nest from dried grass, string and old rags and then converts it into a snug home by lining it with feathers or any other soft material. True 'early birds', the pair ensconce themselves together in the nest on chilly winter nights thus using little unnecessary energy in keeping warm and consequently needing proportionately less food – which is scarce during winter at any rate. In the arid areas where these birds live, the first rains of summer trigger a flush of insect life and breeding can begin at once in the waiting nest. The Cape Sparrow in this way manages to steal a march on time and over a single season will produce several broods.

138 Brilliant yellow eyes, such as those of the Cape Glossy Starling, are characteristic of many members of this family.

139 A 'murmuration' of Cape Glossy Starlings – a most expressive term for an assembly of these loquacious birds! Heads down, birds when drinking are at their most vulnerable. Elephant had knocked down this tree beside a pan and the starlings used it as a noisy half-way perch between the sanctuary of the bush and the water.

140

141

140 Yellow-billed Oxpeckers clamber nimbly over an impassive Sable Antelope. These birds are 'host specific' – they limit their attention to one or two particular groups of animals, depending on the 'hairiness' of the host. Their preference is for animals like the buffalo that are relatively short-haired, while the Red-billed Oxpecker chooses more hirsute hosts.

141 A protruding tuft of red ox-hair tells a tale. A glance at the oxpecker's nest immediately identifies the bird's host as it will crop the animal's hair to line its nesting-hole.

142 Hunters resent the Grey Lourie's 'Go-away' cry that alerts bird and beast to approaching danger.

143 Social Weavers take a rest from nest-building.

144 Work in progress, the partially finished chamber in the centre is just one of the many that honeycomb the Social Weavers' dwelling.

145 The Yellow-throated Sparrow has found a niche no other bird appears to be using. It creeps all over tree trunks searching for highly cryptic mantids camouflaged against the bark.

146 By preparing their untidy nest and sleeping in it during winter, this pair of Cape Sparrows will be ready to begin breeding as soon as the new season begins. Prolific breeders, they will rear several broods before the season is over.

146

Cape Robin

Of all the many so-called robins, 'Jan Frederick' – as the Cape Robin is known colloquially – is the commonest and most widespread. These birds live in pairs, each in its own territory, but some are unable to claim any area as specifically their own and must exist as vagrants among their more successful rivals. Its claim established, the robin remains within its own confined territory, and ringed birds have been recaptured in the same place after intervals of ten years or more. For breeding, it seeks privacy, building its loosely woven grass-and-bark nest in thick bush often on the bank of a stream where it may skulk, hidden by ferns or other undergrowth. It also nests in tree-holes, rock-crevices or in up-turned plant-pots or in forks of trees, its two to four eggs sometimes being rudely ejected by the usurping chick of the Red-crested Cuckoo.

The Robin Redbreast, immortalised by English Christmas cards, is in fact no relation to the Cape Robin which belongs to the thrush sub-family, but the two birds are alike not only in colouring but in their excellence as songsters. 'Jan Frederick' is the Cape Robin's normal call; his song is high, clear and melodious and, when so inclined, he can bewilder the listener by mimicking a wide variety of other birds.

Arrow-marked Babbler

Arrow-marked Babblers are highly gregarious birds, small parties foraging in the undergrowth. They poke about among dead leaves and debris in search of crickets, cockroaches and spiders, hopping vigorously to flush out their victims. Their flight is interspersed with short glides and, when disturbed, they quickly rise into the trees. Hidden from one another by branches and leaves, they keep in touch with grating but subdued calls which each bird answers in turn as if quietly swearing at its fellows. At the least alarm they burst into a vociferous chorus, the harsh sound reaching a crescendo, after which they quietly withdraw.

Although they are birds of the tropics, Arrow-marked Babblers are found as far south as the Transvaal and northern Natal. Between October and January they build their cup-shaped nests of sticks and grass in the veld. These are lined with rootlets and here the female lays three to four pale blue eggs. The Arrow-marked Babbler sometimes finds itself foster-parent to a young Striped-breasted Cuckoo which it rears together with its own chicks.

Helmet Guinea-fowl

All over Africa south of the Sahara, except where there is true desert or evergreen forest, the Helmet Guinea-fowl lives. It is not indigenous to the Karoo or south-west Cape, but on being introduced, adapted itself to these regions successfully wherever man has settled and even makes its home in large suburban gardens.

Except when breeding, guinea-fowl live in flocks, foraging together on the ground and taking refuge in trees when roosting or pursued by predators. Their social structure is highly organised. Dominant males, their wings rucked up high to proclaim status, endlessly chivvy the rest of the flock. Officious as sergeant-majors, they literally rule the roost. They are generally regarded as cautious and cunning birds and are notoriously noisy when alarmed. The two main calls are a loud, harsh, 'Chuck! Chuck!' alarm call and an equally strident 'Buckwheat! Buckwheat!' that the female uses during the breeding season to solicit a suitable mate.

At this time, guinea-fowl pair off but the flock does not disintegrate as the non-breeding birds remain together with the larger group. The males often become extremely aggressive and chase one another about on the ground, scurrying in characteristic guinea-fowl fashion. There are usually six to eight eggs in the nest – a scrape in the ground well-hidden under a bush or hedge – but several females may contribute and increase the number to 30 or more. The parent bird is a close and determined sitter and will remain doggedly on its eggs until it is almost underfoot or – if nesting in a lucerne field – overtaken by a mowing machine.

Helmet Guinea-fowl have incurred the wrath of farmers by digging up newly-planted grain but they compensate for this by eating large numbers of insect pests. In South West Africa they were accused of breaking mealie plants to get at the seeds and a cry went up that guinea-fowl should be destroyed. Investigation revealed, however, that the broken plants were infested with stalk-borers, which were what the bird was after, and the farmers changed their opinion.

For epicures, the guinea-fowl makes good eating and provides excellent sport for hunters. In Natal alone 25 000 are shot in a single season but, at once wary and prolific, the Helmet Guinea-fowl holds its own in spite of the pressure put on it by hunters and certain often misguided agriculturists.

Red-crested Korhaan

The most spectacular characteristic of the Red-crested Korhaan is its courting display. It rises directly into the air, then suddenly topples over and drops, spreading its wings to break its fall just before reaching the ground. Only during the breeding season is there a chance of seeing the male's conspicuous red crest – the rusty cinnamon nape feathers erect in a fine display.

The Red-crested Korhaan is fast and silent on the wing but on the ground it utters a clear far-carrying call which rises in volume for half a minute and then fades away to silence. Curiously, it is extremely difficult to locate the bird's position from the call despite its distinctive quality for the Red-crested Korhaan is one of nature's finest ventriloquists – useful in such a noisy bird whose voice would otherwise be an instant give-away as far as predators are concerned.

Queleas

The small size of the Red-billed Quelea is in no way related to its destructive capabilities for this bird, known aptly as the avian locust, has been declared an international African pest. Indeed, it is in swarms rather than flocks that queleas assemble, often darkening the sky as they approach and numbering thousands, if not millions, of individual birds.

The quelea feeds exclusively on seeds and, to some extent, it was the agricultural revolution that followed the invention of the tractor that contributed to its incredible increase in range and numbers. Vast tracts of country were opened up, providing the quelea with food, and it took to nesting in tree plantations where there had previously been rolling grasslands. Today regular burning of the veld to encourage fresh growth yields a veritable glut of young seed-heads on which the quelea can feed its chicks. In a single year this bird has been responsible for the destruction of the equivalent of 500 000 bags of cereal in South Africa alone, and desperate efforts to reduce the quelea population have proved in vain.

A quelea may start breeding when a few months old, usually laying only two eggs at a time but, to put this in perspective, a single colony may number as many as a million individual nests and sprawl over an area four kilometres long and one wide.

In pursuit of young grass seed-heads for its chicks, the bird moves according to the rains, and when season and site are suitable, the swarm stops to breed. Nests are piled in thorn trees and are sometimes packed so densely that branches break under the strain. Now every predator in the area – vulture, marabou, eagle, hawk, jackal, wild cat and snake – turns its attention to the vast colony but, no matter how concentrated they are, they can destroy no more than a fraction of the eggs and nestlings before breeding is over and the birds move on. They fly over great distances – a bird ringed in South West Africa was recovered in Malawi – and when they settle to drink at a river a crocodile has been known to raise its snout from the water and gulp several queleas in a single mouthful.

Agricultural departments have now given up the unequal struggle to destroy or even decimate this bird. There are huge colonies hidden in remote areas of southern Africa and before these can be poisoned they have to be found – by which time the birds are on the move once more. One fairly effective method of destroying local colonies is aerial spraying at night when the birds come together. However, children often pick up and eat the poisoned birds and there has been some outcry over the matter. The authorities now direct their efforts to driving flocks from roosts or nesting sites near vulnerable crops and in this they have been more successful.

Gabar Goshawk

Small birds in woodlands and savannah dread the Gabar Goshawk for this is one of their most deadly predators. Lurking in trees, especially near a water-hole, this fierce bird seizes its prey in a sudden dash and once, in the Wankie National Park, I saw a Gabar Goshawk make two kills in about 15 minutes. Like all raptors, it catches its victim in its powerful claws and the strong grip, common to all birds of prey, probably suffocates the creature if it has not already been pierced by the goshawk's sharp talons.

The Gabar is found all over southern Africa, with the exception of the south-west. Trees are necessary to it for nesting and as ambushes, but these need not be particularly tall or dense. However, the nests of this and many other goshawks are often adorned by spiders' webs which make them all but invisible from the ground – despite their size. Of course the tantalizing question is, which came first? Did the Gabar build its nest and the spider follow, or did the bird choose that particular tree because of its other tenant? The answer is uncertain and the question remains puzzling.

147 A dramatic white arrow-shaped splash on the Cape Robin's head helps direct its aim when pecking at insects.

Woodpeckers

The woodpecker family is a particularly interesting one. Its members have evolved distinctive characteristics that ensure their place in the forest and are perfectly adapted to its very specialised feeding niches. Gripping the trunk with sharp claws splayed two forward and two back, the woodpecker climbs along the trunks of trees tapping the bark with its strong beak. As it taps it listens, and as soon as it hears that the area beneath the bark is hollow, it chips away to find ants or insects hiding below. Now the woodpecker's most remarkable feature, its tongue, comes into play. It is extraordinarily long, worm-like and mobile. Retracted, it lies in a coil that first reaches to the back of the bird's skull and then curls forward along the inside of the cranium and finally curves around the bird's eye. This is a most versatile tool. A thick mucous covering from special glands at the base of the tongue makes it a sticky trap for ants and termites. Bristles and barbs at the tip capture bulky insects and by neatly retracting it the woodpecker despatches its victim with little fuss.

Constant tapping on wood is a stressful occupation and the woodpecker has evolved various anatomical refinements to cope with and absorb some of the shock. Specially stiffened tail-feathers brace the entire body of the bird as it hammers away; but it is the head that receives most strain. The slender neck is extremely muscular and the head itself is large and equipped with shock-absorbers in the form of thickened areas of bone, air pockets and fleshy cushions.

In the course of feeding, the woodpecker's chisel-like beak is not called upon to work as hard as when digging a nest-hole in solid wood. Then, the full force of the blows is tremendous and the sound reverberates through the forest. At other times the sound of beak on wood serves to keep members of the species in touch with one another, hidden as they are by the dense foliage of their dappled habitat and their own very cryptic colouring.

148 A specially stiffened tail braces the Golden-tailed Woodpecker as it taps away loose bark from a Knob-thorn Acacia in search of insects. As the bird taps, so it listens for hollows beneath the bark which may hide termites, ants or other insects. Once it comes upon a likely spot the bird gives a few smart raps with its straight strong beak and then its remarkable tongue comes into play. Long, worm-like and amazingly mobile it flicks out, capturing small items like ants on its sticky tip, and larger prey on the bristly barbed end. Then the tongue is neatly retracted and the meal despatched without further ado.

149 My patience was rewarded when this Arrow-marked Babbler eventually came out of the front entrance to its nest. Four or five other members of this babbler's family shared the same tree trunk but insisted on using another exit and remained tantalizingly out of range of the camera.

148

149

Lanner Falcon

Fearsome enemy of the quelea – and of all small birds – is the Lanner, though it will also eat lizards and insects, particularly locusts. Beautiful, bold and deadly, the Lanner, with its long wings, is so swift in the air that few birds can match it for speed. The natural conclusion is, that with power and velocity on its side, this bird hunts by snatching up its prey from flocks of small birds; however, the quelea, for example, eludes the predator by constantly moving and by using other surprisingly effective ploys. Queleas travel in dense flocks, often numbering thousands, if not millions, of small birds and the Lanner dare not dive among the milling birds for fear of injury. Therefore it must wait at the edges, eyes alert for stragglers, and only when it sights one separated slightly from the main body does it make its kill. To hasten this it constantly harries the quelea, dive bombing, disturbing and intimidating them. Because the Lanner feeds mainly on the weak, maimed and sick birds, it serves to weed out bad genetic stock from the gene-pool – only the fittest quelea survive to breed again.

Shaft-tailed Whydah

In the breeding season the male Shaft-tailed Whydah presents an ungainly sight with his bobbing flight and spectacular sweeping tail. He is usually accompanied by numerous females and immature birds, and makes a great show of chasing off any unwelcome males. These birds are parasites to the Violet-eared Waxbill, the chicks being so similar to those of the host that the foster-parent cannot distinguish between them. Even the interiors of the mouths of waxbill and whydah match exactly and stimulate the identical feeding instinct in the adult whydah. The male Shaft-tailed Whydah even goes so far as to imitate the song of the Violet-eared Waxbill, though for exactly what purpose no one knows.

Common Waxbill

The lively, bustling Common Waxbill nests on or near the ground, building a ball of grass which is well-hidden in the undergrowth. As incubation proceeds a second, smaller nest is added on top of the first; this used to be known as 'the cock's nest' for it was believed that the male used it for roosting. In fact, the true purpose of the smaller nest is to act as an overflow nursery into which some of the chicks move as they mature. The capacity of the original nest is sometimes further strained by the Pin-tailed Whydah which may add its egg to the clutch; when this happens the Common Waxbill is obliged to hatch and rear the parasite chick in addition to its own.

150 If anything, the White-rumped Babbler is an even noisier bird than the Arrow-marked, which it resembles in size and colouring except for its white rump.

151 What female Angola Thrush could resist this male in his fine breeding-attire – powder-blue head set off against russet breast?

150

151

152 Dawn belongs to the birds. At a water-hole at Etosha Pan, Helmet Guinea-fowl scurry and scuttle, raising a fine film of dust.

153

153 One of nature's finest ventriloquists, the Red-crested Korhaan whose far-carrying cry seems to come from everywhere at once, confusing man and predator alike.

154 Swarming queleas darken the evening sky as they go to roost.

155 Disturbed by my approach, Red-billed Quelea take off from a bush which I estimate held some 10 000 densely-packed birds.

156 Hiding-in-a-crowd, queleas make a difficult target for the Lanner Falcon soaring above. Not daring to plunge into the dense mass of birds for fear of injury, the Lanner must wait for stragglers and, to keep the queleas on the move, it provides endless disturbances, dive-bombing and intimidating them with its presence. Inadvertently the Lanner applies selective pressure to weed out the weak, maimed or sick from the flock – improving the genetic stock in the process.

157 A Gabar Goshawk glowers from its cobweb-festooned nest. The dark area about the bird's eyes is found in many raptors and may well share a common principle with the cockpit shields of modern high-altitude aircraft. These covers are tinted a matt black to cut down the dazzle of the sun, and it is probable that the shadowy area on these birds serves the same purpose.

Fiscal Shrike

Its names – Butcherbird, Jacky Hangman and Fiscal Shrike – all indicate something of the unpopularity of this small predator whose methods of dealing with victims bear a close resemblance to those of the *fiskaal* – an official of the Dutch East India Company – with malefactors. Its small, strong hawk-like beak, hooked in the manner of a raptor, is able to deal not only with insects but also with frogs, lizards and even small birds which it sometimes impales, whether dead or alive, on thorns or barbed wire when not immediately required.

The Fiscal Shrike is a strongly territorial bird, each pair driving other Fiscals from their preserve. Even their own offspring are not exempt from this: as soon as they are sufficiently mature the parent-birds make it perfectly clear that they must move off and fend for themselves.

Though most share black and white plumage, the shrikes of Africa appear to have evolved from two different ancestors. Those related to the European Shrike are characterized by a guttural voice and decidedly unkempt nest-building habits; those related to the warblers are immediately identified by their melodious song and neat well-constructed nests.

Black-eyed Bulbul

Wherever there is wooded country throughout southern Africa, the Black-eyed Bulbul is found. Bold and friendly, it is easily located from its cheerful characteristic call which becomes particularly agitated whenever a snake, predator or even cat appears. Indeed, this bird is recognised by birds and animals alike as an indicator of danger and all heed its warning.

Hornbills

In southern Africa, the Grey Hornbill occupies an ecological niche equivalent to that of the toucan in South America. It is a tree-nester *par excellence* for the female further ensures her already safe position in the protected nest by walling herself in with a mixture of mud and debris cemented together with saliva.

While incubating the eggs, she moults all her wing and tail feathers and depends upon the male to bring food to her and to her chicks. The chief danger of this peculiar breeding-habit is that the female and her offspring are doomed if anything happens to the male, for she remains flightless until her plumage reappears about three weeks after the eggs hatch. She then breaks out of the nest to assist her mate in feeding the young which, strangely enough, immediately set about rebuilding the wall round the entrance until it is as good and safe as ever.

Alan Kemp observed an astonishing event while monitoring hornbills in the Kruger National Park. A female hornbill had set up her nest in a tree-hole with a rather small entrance, and while she incubated and hatched her clutch the cambium layer of the tree began to grow across the hole threatening to seal her in. She subsequently managed to squeeze out herself but her chicks were not ready to fly and were eventually doomed to death in the tree trunk where their skeletons remain to this day.

The Ground Hornbill is a turkey-sized bird as curious in its appearance as it is in its habits. It takes short steps for so big a bird and this results in its characteristic waddling gait, like the roll of a deep-sea sailor ashore; and its ponderous flight and surprising eye-lashes are other oddities of this, the largest of the hornbills.

Intensely territorial, it has a deep booming voice with which it proclaims its own home-range which may be several hundred hectares in extent and must include open country where it can feed on insects, frogs, small reptiles and mice, and trees in which it roosts and nests. For the Ground Hornbill, despite its large size, still nests in tree-hollows though it does not, as the smaller species do, wall up the female while she incubates and rears the young. In fact, she is sufficiently liberated to leave the nest from time to time to forage for herself. Unfortunately the Ground Hornbill suffers from a serious disadvantage where man is concerned. Alarmed by the arrival of human intruders, the female hastily deserts the nest, trampling her eggs in the process. Owing to her sheer size, they are generally crushed and destroyed, and for this reason the nests should be protected by law.

Familiar with the Ground Hornbill's resounding voice, tribal Africans maintain that the female declares: 'I am going, I am going, I am going to my relations!' And to this the male replies: 'You can go, you can go, you can go to your relations!' But certainly there is no truth in the interpretation of the calls as an indication of matrimonial disharmony!

158 In a colony containing millions of nests, a male Red-billed Quelea delivers a beakful of seeds to its young.

Scarlet-breasted Sunbird

Sunbirds are a family of African and Asian birds which fill an ecological niche equivalent to that occupied by the humming-birds of America. The Scarlet-breasted, one of the larger species found in southern Africa, prefers veld to woodland and is a frequent visitor to gardens, particularly if they are bright with flowers.

This is an active, restless and pugnacious bird. It darts about from one flower to another, taking nectar and the insects it attracts, but should any other sunbird be bold enough to show an interest in its private food-supply, it rapidly chases off the intruder. But the Scarlet-breasted Sunbird does not only feed from flowers: it also forages for ants, grubs and crickets on the ground, picks caterpillars from leaves and catches flying termites in the air. Spiders, too, are a favourite dish.

Though it moves about to some extent in search of flowering trees and shrubs, the Scarlet-breasted Sunbird seldom goes far. Sometimes the small, metallic green Klaas's Cuckoo lays its eggs in the sunbird's nest and when the interloper hatches, it evicts the eggs and young of its foster-parents in order to secure their undivided attention for itself.

Flowering plants, such as the proteas and ericas of South Africa, offer nectar to birds with long, curved beaks. Delving deep into the blossoms with beak and extended hollow tongue, the sunbirds' heads are dusted with pollen which they carry from bloom to bloom as they feed, fertilizing the plants in the process.

Fiscal Flycatcher

At first glance the Fiscal Flycatcher might be mistaken for a Fiscal Shrike, not only because the two birds look alike but because both have the habit of perching conspicuously on telephone poles. But to confuse the birds would do an injustice to the Flycatcher for it does not share the Fiscal Shrike's notorious habits of preying upon and impaling small birds and reptiles. Yet the resemblance is not merely fortuitous: it is an example of the phenomenon of 'mimicry' for the Fiscal Shrike is a tough and savage bird and it is much to the flycatcher's advantage to be mistaken for it, since other birds are glad to leave it alone.

Black Sunbird

Black Sunbirds feed their young almost exclusively on spiders which they sometimes pluck from the apparent safety of their webs, though the males spend so much time chasing other sunbirds away from the food-source that it seems surprising that they ever achieve a square meal. Female Black Sunbirds occasionally take advantage of the male's carefully guarded food supply: in a game of bluff and counter-bluff she convinces him that she is interested in becoming his mate when in fact her attentions are not at all honourable. She quite willingly prostitutes herself for the sake of a meal and then takes off for new pastures.

Lesser Honeyguide

The Lesser Honeyguide is so well adapted to parasitizing that the chick, on hatching, has powerful hooks on its beak with which it kills the host's young. Once the undivided attention of the foster-parent is assured, the hooks gradually disappear.

Barbets are favourite foster-parents for honeyguide chicks. The honeyguide pair work as a team: the male flushes the nesting barbet from its tree-hole and while the barbet tries to chase it off, the female honeyguide loses no time in entering the nest and adding her eggs to the clutch. However, in the brief time available and restricted by the tree-hole nest's perpendicular walls, she cannot, as the cuckoo does, help guarantee her chick's survival by dumping out any of the barbet's clutch. It is imperative, therefore, that her chick itself be equipped to deal with the barbet chicks— hence the beak hooks. After the young honeyguide has killed its rivals, the adult barbets remove the corpses, unaware of the treachery being enacted in the gloom of the nest and the honeyguide nestling helps ensure its eventual survival by cutting competition. In a further adaptation to its foster home the young honeyguide sports special claws that it uses to climb the walls of the nest and finally escape the tree-hole when the time comes to fly.

Wood Hoopoe

Intleki'Bafazi – or 'laughing women' – is the Xhosa name for the Wood Hoopoe which makes an incessant chattering sound, usually started by a single bird and then taken up by the entire flock. This is essentially a veld bird which scrambles about on trees, propping itself against the trunk with its tail and probing deep into the bark for grubs and insects with its long beak. Wood Hoopoes move about in parties and the family-bond is so strong that the feeding of the young, in their tree-hole nests, is not the responsibility of the parents alone but of the whole flock. But nest-sanitation is unknown to the Wood Hoopoe whose 'procreant cradle' soon becomes foul-smelling and the bird itself, with its strong meaty smell, is certainly no nosegay.

159 Competing for sheer brilliance of colour, a glittering Scarlet-breasted Sunbird sips nectar from the slender throats of aloe blossoms.

160 Though it gives the impression of being perpetually busy, the Orange-breasted Waxbill avoids home-building if possible. It prefers to take over a nest from some other more industrious bird – a weaver, widow or bishop – and then furnishes it cosily, lining it with feathers, grass-heads and other soft material.

161 Trailing tail-feathers in the breeze, a male Shaft-tailed Whydah sports his breeding attire.

162 Feathers puffed up against the morning chill, a Common Waxbill perches amid seed-heads dusted with dew.

163 The origin of its name clearly visible, the Cut-throat Finch is not in fact a finch at all, but a waxbill.

183

161

162

163

164 Less than 100 years ago Johannesburg was merely rolling veld. Trees grew mainly near rivers and streams and were the habitat of the Crested Barbet. Today the thousands of trees planted on the Witwatersrand have extended this bird's habitat so that it is one of the most common species in the area.

165 Hovering outside a barbet's tree-hole, a male Lesser Honeyguide tries to entice the sitting bird out so that his mate waiting near by can slip in and deposit her eggs – a process that will take her only seconds to accomplish. People who have mist-netted honeyguides for ringing have been astonished to find an egg deposited in their hands within moments of holding the bird.

164

166 Black, white and red were the colours of the Old German Empire and for this reason the German-speaking people of South West Africa have nick-named the Crimson-breasted Shrike, *Reichsvogel*. While cobwebs are a common nesting material, the origins of the neat strips of bark that make up this shrike's nest prove a mystery.

167 A mini-predator, the Fiscal Shrike has a hawk-like beak – the only visible sign that it is anything but a gentle little bird. Feeding on frogs, insects, lizards and even small birds, it is a successful hunter notorious for its occasional practice of impaling victims on thorns or barbed wire until needed for a meal.

168 Tail braced firmly against the tree trunk, a Grey Hornbill passes food to his mate (the tip of her beak is just visible) sealed with her clutch in the tree-hole nest. While incubating her eggs in this hot confined space, she moults all her wing and tail feathers and is totally dependent on the male for food. Should anything happen to him during this period, mother and her chicks will perish in their cloistered nest.

169 Recognised by bird and beast as a danger indicator, the Black-eyed Bulbul's characteristic call rings out a warning whenever a predator is about. It is often the first to spot the intruder simply because it is so widespread that little passes it by.

170 One warning look from the cold blue eyes of the Ground Hornbill and the intruder is on his guard. The age of this aggressive bird can be judged by the shade of red in the naked skin areas of the adult: the older the hornbill the deeper the colouring.

167

189

171

172

171 This Chin-spot Battis's nest, built in a forked tree-branch, is cleverly concealed by a covering of lichen over a tidy bowl of fibres and other woody material. Sexual dimorphism is present in these birds: the male is entirely black and white but the female has a neat brick-red chin-spot and breast-band.

172 At first glance the Fiscal Flycatcher might be mistaken for a Fiscal Shrike, but its neat nest and melodious call immediately reveal its different ancestry.

173 Only its startlingly red eye-ring distinguishes the Red-eyed Bulbul from the Black.

174 A young Wood Hoopoe stretches to take a morsel of food brought by its parent to the foul-smelling tree-hole nest.

175 An adult Black Sunbird carefully removes a faecal sac from its nest. The nestlings of various birds produce their faeces in a fine membranous container and, where nesting is concerned, this is a hygienic necessity.

Birds of the Riverine Forest

Forest avifauna may be grouped into ecological categories according to height between ground and tree-top at which the birds function. There are birds of the forest floor, guinea-fowl for instance, that scurry among the undergrowth, feeding on grubs, worms and beetles, and rarely rising from their ground-level habitat. In the middle 'storey' live flycatchers, warblers, woodpeckers, barbets and so on, that hawk insects in the air or take caterpillars and insects from trunks and leaves. Finally there are the fruit-eaters of the forest canopy and the predators who keep vigilant watch from their tree-top look-outs for likely targets down below. Although each species operates on its own level as it were, there is a certain amount of interplay. Guinea-fowl flap into the branches to roost and hide; woodpeckers may descend to the ground to feed and predators swoop down to hunt.

Forest birds are relatively long-lived. In their stable environment many live to a ripe old age – in bird terms, anyway – and a Heuglin's Robin may reach ten years or more, which is quite exceptional for a bird its size. Together with this longevity and peaceful existence comes a less frenetic breeding rate and birds of the forest rear their young in leisurely fashion. Indeed, life generally is not as precarious and exposed as that of birds in other habitats and, apart from man, little threatens the forest sanctuary.

Black-collared Barbet

In her nesting hole the female Black-collared Barbet lays three or four plain white eggs. Only species that lay in open nests need resort to cryptically coloured and patterned eggs: those of hole-nesters like the barbet lie hidden in darkness. What is more, in the sanctuary of the tree trunk, the stage between hatching and fledging is longer than that of open-nesting species whose chicks are easy prey for roving predators.

Therefore, among open-nesting birds there is a premium on rearing the chicks to fledgling stage as quickly as possible: extending the process unnecessarily would only further endanger the already vulnerable young. Hole-nesters have the advantage of physical protection and their offspring develop more slowly, placing less of a burden on the parents that must forage far and wide to feed them. This also affects 'family planning' – encouraging parents to produce more young at a time and breed less often, for the brood seems to have a better guarantee of survival than, say, those of open-nesting birds. Hole-nesting, however, is not entirely fail-safe. For instance, the Lesser Honeyguide presents a very real and recognised threat against which the barbets put up a vigorous defence.

To illustrate this point, I made a fascinating observation a few years ago. Quite by chance I discovered a honeyguide chick in a barbet nest and saw that the adult barbets were feeding it on seeds, a very different diet from the one that the mature honeyguide enjoys. Convinced that this should be put on

record, I perched the nestling just outside the entrance to the tree-hole whereupon the adult barbets savagely attacked it. Needless to say, I hurriedly replaced it in the nest and then watched in amazement as, minutes later, the barbets placidly resumed feeding it. Apparently, in the dark of the nesting-hole the adult barbets were oblivious to the true identity of the chick, and only in open daylight did they recognise it for what it was – and reacted accordingly!

This episode illustrates the incongruous attitude that some birds have to their nests and young. The nest and its contents are perceived as a whole, and as long as they are not physically separated the adults view them as a single entity to be cared for and protected – even if, as in this case, the chicks are foreign implants.

176 Still ensconced in its nest in the bole of a dead tree, a Black-collared Barbet makes sure that no predator is in sight before venturing out. This species excavates its own nesting holes using its powerful broad beak to rip away soft wood and bark.

177 Strutting like a goose-stepping soldier, an Angola Mourning Dove fixes a bright eye on a promising feeding ground below.

176

Robins

The Caruso of forest birds everywhere – including the North American Mockingbird and the celebrated Nightingale – is Heuglin's Robin. Wherever there are tropical forests in southern Africa, this bird's song is heard – rich in tone, loud in volume and varied in vocabulary. It also has a fine ear and if one listens carefully the songs of other birds that share the forest habitat can often be heard woven into the melody.

During the breeding season this bird is highly territorial and song plays an important role in proclaiming nesting areas and deterring would-be rivals. So spontaneously does this robin respond to song, that when I played back a tape-recording of its own voice, the bird perched proudly on the machine and chased away any other creature that approached. Strong, rich song is a feature common to many birds of the forest. Extensive repertoires serve a multitude of purposes: for instance, in the shade of the forest male and female often depend on song rather than visual contact to keep in touch and their delightful duetting has been the subject of much research. Feeding pairs transmit information about fruitful areas and with their calls birds warn all and sundry when predators appear. Even more sophisticated are those birds that mimic the calls of different species to help keep them away and limit competition in their own territories.

Like the Cape Robin, the White-throated is a frequent victim of the Red-chested Cuckoo or *Piet-my-vrou*. The cuckoo adds its egg to the White-throated Robin's clutch and as soon as the young cuckoo is hatched it promptly proceeds to rid the nest of the eggs and other young. Its back is well adapted to this tyranny for there is a convenient hollow into which, one by one, it manages to load its victims. It then climbs backwards up the side of the nest and neatly tilts its competition over the rim. Usually that is the end of egg or chick which then falls to the ground; but, should the unfortunate chick stick to the edge of the nest, it is still doomed. Apparently, the adult White-throated Robin does not recognise its own chicks when very young, except in the context of the nest and will either remove them as it would a piece of extraneous rubbish or, worse still, ignore them until they die of exposure and hunger. Meanwhile, that voracious parasite the cuckoo reigns supreme assured of its foster-parents' undivided attention. Indeed, their ministrations extend even beyond fledgling stage and they continue to feed it for quite some time after it has left the nest – as they would their own.

178-179 The Crested Guinea-fowl is a bird of the forest floor, searching the ground for millipedes, insects, fruit, roots and bulbs. Surprisingly, monkeys and guinea-fowl are often found together. The monkeys feeding in the trees drop bits of waste food to the fowl waiting below but whether the monkeys are conscious of their role as providers is doubtful. Occasionally one comes upon the entertaining spectacle of monkeys gaily swinging through the tree-tops while guinea-fowl scurry anxiously in their wake.

179

180 Taken from my camp bed, this photograph of a Heuglin's Robin barely conveys the obvious enthusiasm and the glorious sound emitted by this little bird.

181 Most rollers are open-country birds but the Broad-billed is a migrant to southern Africa's dense woodlands and forests. Richly coloured, it has all the roller characteristics: harsh voice, pugnacious disposition and remarkable flying expertise.

180

181

183

184

182 & 184 Decorative and spectacular on the wing with its streaming tail feathers swirling like a piece of ribbon as it pursues an insect, the Paradise Flycatcher is fairly inconspicuous on the nest. Male and female take turns in incubating the clutch, the male's very long tail (lower right photograph) easily distinguishing it from its mate. The nest is small and situated near the end of a thin side-branch of a tree, often over water, so that it is both hard to find and difficult to reach.

183 The Kurrichane Thrush, a relative of the European Blackbird, finds much of its food while it forages swiftly on foot on the forest floor. It was named by the Scottish doctor, explorer and naturalist Andrew Smith who first discovered it in the late 19th century near Kurrichane, the capital of an African tribe in the Western Transvaal.

185 The Boubou Shrike's hungry brood clamours for the colourful wasp the foraging parent has found. In the dense undergrowth the birds keep in touch with cry and answer calls that make a distinctive duet.

185

203

186 In the shelter of a pottery shard, a White-throated Robin ministers to the demanding needs of a Red-chested Cuckoo chick already much larger than its foster-parent.

187-188 The Groundscraper Thrush feeds its ever-hungry chicks on insects which, as its name suggests, it finds by doing a great deal of scratching about on the forest floor. Over the course of a day, food is equally distributed among the three nestlings although feeding reaches a pitch at dawn when hungry stomachs clamour for food after the long night, and at dusk when the parents must satisfy their offsprings' hunger pangs until the following morning.

187   188

Index

Page numbers in bold type refer to photographs

Albatross 33
— Black-browed 33, **35, 37, 38, 39**
— Wandering 33
Babbler, Arrow-marked 166, **169**
— White-rumped **170**
Barbet 182, **187**
— Black-collared 196, **196**
— Crested **186**
Battis, Chin-spot **192**
Bee-eater, Carmine 131, 134, **138, 139**
— Little **145**
Bishop, Red **140**
Bulbul, Black-eyed 180, **190**
— Red-eyed **193**
Buzzard, Augur **128**, 130
— Jackal **129**, 130
Chat, Mountain 130, **132**
Cormorant 13-15, **16, 18, 31**, 102
— Cape **12**, 13-15, **14, 16**
— Crowned **17**
— Reed **15**, 17
— White-breasted **13**, 15, 17
Crake, Black 91-92, **93**
Crane 72
— Blue (Stanley) 72, **74**
— Crowned **69, 70**, 72, **73**
— Wattled 72, **74**
Crow, Pied **157**, 158-159
Cuckoo, Red-crested (Piet-my-Vrou) 166, 198, **204**
— Striped-breasted 166
Dikkop, Water **88**
Dove, Angola Mourning **197**
— Cape Turtle 144, **146, 148**
— Laughing **147**
Duck 76, 81, **83**
— Black 77, 78, 81, **84**
— Knob-billed 78, **81, 82**
— Mallard 76, 78
— White-backed **79**
— White-faced **57, 76, 80**
— Yellowbill **75**, 78
Eagle 120-123, 167
— African Hawk (Bonelli's) 120, **122, 123, 125**
— Bateleur 121-123, **126, 127**
— Black (Verreaux's) 120, **120**, 121, **121**
— Fish 102, **102, 103, 104, 105**
— Tawny 120, **124**
Egret 48
— Cattle (Buff-backed Heron or Tickbird) 48, **49, 50**
— Yellow-billed **52**

Falcon, Lanner 170, **178**
— Pygmy 158
Finch, Cut-throat **185**
— Red-headed 158
Flamingo, 34, **44, 45**
— Greater 34, **46**
— Lesser 34
Flycatcher, Fiscal 182, **192**
— Paradise **202**
Gannet, Cape (cover photograph), **18**, 20-22, **20, 21**
Goose, Pygmy **86**, 88
— Spurwing **87**, 88
Goshawk, Gabar 167, **179**
Guinea-fowl, Crested **198, 199**
— Helmet 166, **172**
Gull, Grey-headed **26, 27**
— Hartlaub's 33
— Kelp 28, **29, 30, 32, 42**
Harrier, African Marsh **106**, 107
Heron 63, 102
— Black-headed **54**
— Green-backed **53**
— Purple **55**, 63
— Squacco **68**
Honeyguide, Lesser 182, **186**, 196
Hoopoe, Wood 182, **193**
Hornbill 131, 180
— Grey 180, **190**
— Ground 123, 180, **191**
Ibis, Bald 64, **67**
— Hermit 64
— Sacred 25, **25**
Jacana, African ('Lily Trotter') **89, 90, 91**, 91
— Lesser **92**
Kingfisher, Giant 98, **99**
— Malachite 98, **98, 100, 101**
Kite, Yellow-billed 112, **113**
Korhaan, Black **137**
— Red-crested 166, **174**
Lourie, Grey ('Go-away Bird') 159, **162**
Lovebird, Rosy-faced 144, 158
Martin, Banded Sand **141**
Mousebird 158
Openbill **62, 83, 87**
Ostrich 110-112, **108, 110, 111**
Owl 150
— Giant Eagle ('Milky') 150, **151, 152**
— Pearl-spotted **154**
— Scops 149, 150, **153**
Oxpecker 159
— Red-billed 159, **161**
— Yellow-billed 159, **161**
Oystercatcher, Black 33, **40**
Parrot, Meyer's 144, **146**

Pelican, White 22-23, **22, 23, 24, 83**
Penguin, Jackass **7,** 8, **9, 10**
Plover, Crowned *(Kiewietjie)* 134, **136**
Quelea, Red-billed 110, 167, 170, **175, 176, 178, 181**
Rail 92
Robin, Cape ('Jan Frederick') 166, **167,** 198
— . Heuglin's 196, 198, **200**
— White-throated 198, **204**
Roller, Broad-billed **201**
— Lilac-breasted (Mzilikazi's) 130, **135**
— Purple 130-131, **136**
— Racket-tailed 130
Saddlebill **64**
Sandgrouse 118
— Double-banded 118
— Namaqua 118, **119**
Shrike, Boubou **203**
— Crimson-breasted *(Reichsvogel)* **188**
— Fiscal (Butcherbird, 'Jacky Hangman') 180, 182, **189**
Skimmer, African **83,** 94, **94,** 95
Sparrow, Cape ('Mossie') 159, **165**
Sparrow, Yellow-throated **164**
Spoonbill **56, 57, 58, 80**
Starling, Cape Gossy **160**
Stork 63
— Marabou 63, **65, 66,** 112, 167
— White **60,** 63
— White-bellied (Abdim's) **59,** 63
— Wood **62,** 63
Sunbird, Black 182, **194**
— Scarlet-breasted 182, **183**

Swallow, Cliff 130, **131**
— Lesser Striped **132**
— White-throated **141**
— Wire-tailed **133**
Teal, Red-bill **81**
Tern 33-34, **41, 42, 44**
— Arctic 33-34
— Caspian 33
— Com-ic 34
— Common 33-34, **41**
— Damara 33
Thrush, Angola **171**
— Groundscraper **205**
— Kurrichane **202**
Vulture 112-115, **117,** 167
— Cape 110, 112, 115, **115**
— Hooded 112, **114,** 115
— Lappet-faced 112, **114,** 115
— White-backed 112, 115, **116**
Wagtail, Cape **96**
Waxbill, Common 170, **185**
— Orange-breasted **184**
— Violet-eared 170
Weaver 158
— Cape **156,** 158
— Red-headed **155,** 158
— Social 158, **162, 163**
Whydah, Pin-tailed 170
— Shaft-tailed 170, **185**
Woodpecker 168
— Golden-tailed **168**